the pacifist's guide to self-flagellation

john larkin

the pacifist's guide to self-flagellation

HODDER

For my family
and in memory of my grandma, Mary Kennedy

A Hodder Book

Published in Australia and New Zealand in 2003
by Hodder Headline Australia Pty Limited
(A member of the Hodder Headline Group)
Level 22, 201 Kent Street, Sydney NSW 2000
Website: www.hha.com.au

National Library of Australia
Cataloguing-in-Publication data

Larkin, John, 1963- .
   The pacifist's guide to self-flagellation.

   ISBN 0 7336 1396 9.

   1. Larkin, John, 1963- - Childhood and youth. 2. Authors -
Australia - Biography. 3. Children - New South Wales -
Sydney - Social life and customs. 4. Sydney (N.S.W.) -
Social life and customs. I. Title.

A823.3

Text design and typesetting by Bookhouse, Sydney
Printed in Australia by Griffin Press, Adelaide

Author's Note

The following events are real, or at least as real as I remember them. I have changed the names of certain people to protect the innocent—namely me. Other characters will appear to be the work of fiction and that's largely because they're not. I didn't attend school with anyone called Pugsley Porksworth, David Dawkins or Roland Roundbutt, but they are no less real for my having forgotten their names.

Three brief excerpts from this book have previously appeared in a slightly different form: *Canberra Calling* was first published in my short story collection *Bite Me!* as *Dead Numbat Walking*. The side-garden cricket rules appeared in my teen novel *Pizza Features*, and one of the paragraphs in the chapter titled *The Red Rattler and the Bandsaw* was published in my travel narrative *Larkin about in Ireland*.

Writing is a form of self-flagellation
—William Styron

England

I

Life, Death, Needle & Thread

You shouldn't be reading this. I wasn't meant to be here this long. The god that determines the fate of babies had apparently decided my stay on earth was going to be short, but fate hadn't reckoned on a mother whose obstinate nature was, I suppose, passed on to me.

With one child already lost to meningitis, she was not about to offer up another, no matter which god was asking. So when I was struck down with the same illness that had claimed my older brother and Death reached out its hand, it was rapped soundly over the knuckles. My mother had given me life and now went about insisting that I keep it. She never let me out of her sight. I wasn't so much tied to her apron strings as sewn.

I was born in the South Yorkshire mining town of Maltby in 1963. The only other significant event that year was John F Kennedy's ill-fated tour of Dallas. His death, tragic though it was, had little impact on Maltby apart from the fact that there were more than the usual number of Johns and Jacquelines born that year. Many years later in Australia I was delighted to find that the Kennedy mystique had touched places more remote than Maltby, when I met a tall gorgeous, sophisticated Jacqueline of my own, who eventually agreed to marry me.

My birth date was 20 April, a birthday I share with only one famous person: Adolf Hitler. When I discovered this as a twelve-year-old I was mortified and sometimes woke in a cold sweat, having dreamt that I was his reincarnation. The fact that I had a full complement of testicles and was not a short-arsed Austrian psychopath brought little relief, though. And, like Damien of the *Omen* films, who was absolutely horrified when he found the mark of the beast, 666, tattooed on his scalp, I was afraid that one day I would suddenly develop the urge to grow a moustache, take up painting, become a Nazi, be kind to animals and invade Queensland. Statistics told me that one in every 365.25 people who were born after the Caesars and Pope Gregory had stopped mucking around with the calendar, were also born on 20 April, but I was twelve years old and determined to hang on to any neurosis I could.

My parents, Pat and Brendan, of Irish Catholic stock, insist that I was named after the then Pope. But I doubt it. The height of my mother's beehive in photographs at the time suggests that she was a little more sixties than that. Of course, the fact that Pope Paul was in office when my brother Paul came along in 1968 seemed to strengthen their assertion. But the sound of the Mersey beat drifting across the Pennines and the sexual revolution surging up the M1 from London could not have totally bypassed Maltby. Less devout than my father, my mother was obviously thinking of Paul McCartney when they named my little brother and was no doubt secretly pleased that she had pulled a rather fast one on the old man.

Earlier, in 1961, the Catholic Church had still not anointed a female pope, so my mother was able to be a bit more adventurous with my sister's name. Mercifully, she resisted the temptation to call her baby daughter Doris, Connie, Eartha or Peggy and settled instead on the slightly pious Patricia, which, though hardly exotic, allowed my sister a number of abbreviations. She has been Trish, Pat and Trish again down the years, depending on her mood. Inspired by the Trojan Horse, Paul and I have always called her "Troje".

Meningitis aside, I suppose my first couple of years went smoothly. I apparently gooed and gaaed when I should have, crawled and walked at the appropriate time and just generally got by until my memory started to kick in when I was three. The only lasting family anecdote dated before this was of my hovering between life and death in the hospital. After a particularly eventful night when I took a turn for the worse, Mum woke from a fitful sleep in the chair beside my cot, expecting to find me either marginally on the mend or dead. Instead she found me running up and down the cot, kicking a little soccer ball. With a story like that, it was obviously my destiny to become a world-famous footballer. You could almost hear future commentators bleating the tale to each other as I tucked the winner away at Wembley, 'You couldn't write a script better than that'.

Like most people's, my earliest recollections are fragments and come at me haphazardly, without much context or meaning, a bit like a Peter Greenaway film.

Our home at number 8 Highfield Park was a large three-bedroom semi-detached council house with a big back lawn and its own garage—all of which Mum and Dad kept immaculate.

Most of my early memories are associated with this house: Dad coming home from his work as a bus driver and jumping over the brick wall out the front, presumably to impress me—and it did, greatly. Our back lawn with its own little hill and a large bramble patch in the corner that Trish hid in when she had broken yet another house rule that had been designed to prevent me experiencing further loss of blood. Gazing at the watery Yorkshire sun and wondering where it went at night or at the circular window of the house over the road and trying to imagine how the world looked through a round window. Being told by Mum that the cracks in the road leading to the next village of Braithwell were caused by all the dinosaurs under the ground and wondering whether she'd been at the cooking sherry. Staring in disbelief at an aerobatic plane high above and thinking that it was a commercial aircraft in trouble. Hearing the creak of the eighth step that Dad tried hard to avoid each morning in case I got up and pestered him with questions about round windows, dinosaurs, crashing planes, where the sun went at night and the effect of cooking sherry on the mental faculties of mothers.

Invariably he got it wrong and aimed for the ninth step but missed and landed more heavily on the eighth—and I leapt out of bed and raced downstairs to annoy him.

I remember being around people who thought that three-wheel cars were a great idea and would catch on. Probably the same people who believed they were having a hell of a time yelling out, *'Quack Quack Quack!'* when twenty-two was called in bingo and were proud of the fact that they were educated in the school of hard knocks and had earned degrees from the university of life. 'I don't know much, but I'll tell you this for now't.' And I remember the lovely people next door called Uncle Judd and Aunt Doris, who weren't related to us at all but whom I was too young to call simply Judd and Doris.

I also remember wanting to work in the local biscuit factory when I grew up—I wanted the job of eating all the broken biscuits. Feeling upset because I couldn't marry my cousin Jacqueline because she *was* my cousin Jacqueline (please disregard this if you happen to be reading in Kentucky). Being looked after by my grandmother because my mother had to go and work in the stocking factory. Getting drenched under a sheet of water sluiced up by a passing bus and patted dry by a thousand handkerchiefs of well-meaning, community-spirited women and hoping that none of them was carrying a fatal disease, while Mum said, 'If that was your dad I'll bloody murder him!'

Swirls of memories that overlay, intersect and blend with each other and make me dizzy. I need air.

That's better.

My first recollection in which the fragments come together substantially is of an odd incident that apparently took place just after I'd turned three. I would have dismissed it as complete nonsense if it weren't for Trish having the same memory.

A young man had come off his motorbike (though 'come off' is probably not the best verb to explain his being flattened by two tonnes of screaming metal) at the junction of our street, Highfield Park, and Grange Lane, which was the main road to Braithwell. Despite its name, Grange Lane was fairly busy. Starved for enter-tainment—these were people who actively looked forward to the Val Doonican and Andy Williams vari-ety shows in the evenings—everyone rushed from their houses to check out the carnage. People leaned over walls and said things like, 'Eee by gum', 'By eckie thump', 'Oh I know', 'Nice day for it', 'We're thinkin' of guin for a run out to Skegness on Sat'dee. Teck new motor', 'Weather's changing since they started sending up them satellites', and shared slanderous gossip, mostly about who was shagging whom—though they used the curious euphemism, 'run off with'.

There was a bit of a huddle around the man, so we couldn't see any spilt brains or other bodily fluids. I was just about to get seriously bored with the whole busi-ness when a lady from a few houses down waddled past and said, 'He's bleeding quite badly. I'm off to get me needle and thread.'

Both Trish and I recoiled in horror, but Mum didn't hear what the old lady had said. She was busy with her concerns about NASA disrupting global climatic pat-terns with their bloody satellites.

If the poor guy hadn't suffered enough, he now had to endure some strange woman leaning over him with her sewing kit and a copy of the *Wives' Tales Weekly*, "Knit your own Motorcyclist" pattern. I can only hope that mercy prevailed and that either the ambulance arrived or he died before she could decide which stitch to use.

Radiant with ignorance, I didn't realise it at the time, but it was just this sort of pulling together that had won the war—that and a few million heavily armed American, Australian and Allied troops. Yorkshire people have this reputation for being cold, hard and completely devoid of emotion. And it's a reputation that is fully deserved. You might get a handshake and an 'All the best' from your father on your twenty-first birthday, but that would be about it. I've seen women settle disputes with a well-aimed lump of coal, while men have their tear-ducts compulsorily sewn shut when they hit puberty. But if you're down on your luck, have had your leg removed by a combine harvester or rabid dog, have gone into labour in the middle of the high street, or else "come off" your motorcycle and are bleeding to death on the side of the road, that's when Yorkshire people come into their own. I have never encountered more giving or resourceful people in a crisis. Just don't try to hug them by way of a thank you.

I had this brought home to me many years later, when I returned home to Maltby in a last-ditch effort to make it as a professional footballer. Although I'd been playing successfully in the Australian National Soccer League (NSL) I decided to walk away from it and start again at the bottom in England. This was 1985 and the Australian NSL wasn't the fertile breeding ground for

English Premier League clubs that it is now. And, as I was twenty-one, I figured that time was still on my side. My plan was to play in a Sunday pub league and if I was as good as I thought I was, word would get out and scouts from Manchester United, Liverpool, Arsenal, Tottenham Hotspurs and Grimsby Town would soon be beating a path to my door. I said a cheerful farewell to my family at Sydney Airport—my father shook my hand and said, 'All the best'—and I set off on my *Boys' Own* adventure.

I was no sooner off the plane than I was carving up defences for the Maltby Catholic Club first XI under an assumed name. This was partly because my NSL club had refused to grant me a clearance, but mostly because I felt that "John Dempsey" lent me a sort of raffish air. It also gave me the chance to totally reinvent myself. John Dempsey could pirouette on the ball like Rudolf Nureyev on speed. He could slalom down the wing while balancing the ball on his forehead. He would make mincemeat out of the right fullback, centre half and sweeper, all while he appeared not to give a damn. This guy did not give a shit. He was even considering dreadlocks. But then, in my fifth game—the very day I was approached by a scout from Leeds United (or a man in an anorak, at any rate)—I damaged my knee beyond repair and that, as they say, was that. Not only did my team and some of the opposition come and visit me in hospital, but both teams organised a whip-round to cover me while I was off work, even though I was technically unemployed.

Fast forward to an over-30s game in Sydney on a cold winter's night in 1996. I'm bounding down the wing—tragically now more like Pavarotti than Nureyev—when my Achilles tendon snaps and I am again carted off to hospital in agony. Apart from my old friend Steve Campbell (who, figuring I was the victim of foul play, went about systematically ploughing the opposition into the dirt) I never heard from any of my so-called teammates again. I'll tell you this for now't: that would never have happened in Yorkshire.

I knew none of this as I stood gawping at the broken motorcyclist—if I had, I probably would have taken up chess instead. I just thought that the old woman was mad. Though that's probably only my memory playing tricks. Three-year-olds think that grownups know everything—even those who own three-wheel cars and say, 'By eckie thump'. They don't, of course, but you have to become a grownup first to realise it. And I had a long, long way to go.

2

Man of Granite, Woman of the Old West

Grandma and Grandad Kennedy lived in one of the old miners' houses at the bottom of Highfield Park on Nelson Road.

For some reason we always entered their house from the lane behind. Even when we found ourselves out the front we would walk up the small alley (which we called a "jennel") to the back door. I suppose the people of Nelson Road were so used to entering other people's homes by the tradesman's entrance that they saw no reason to alter the practice when it came to their own. And when every couple of years or so the council painter came along to apply a fresh coat to the front door, he was painting over doors that had long since been painted shut.

The houses on Nelson Road were mostly occupied by miners and their families and, even to a small boy, seemed claustrophobic: enclosed rooms, narrow stair-cases, hemmed-in kitchens. It was as if they had been designed for little people.

My grandma, Mary, hailed from Thryberg and was my only English grandparent, while Tom, my grandfather, came from Sligo on the west coast of Ireland. They must have bred them tough in that part of the world because he remains to this day the hardest person I have ever encountered. His hands were like slabs of concrete wrapped in weathered hide and his shoulders so broad that Trish and I could ride up there together— one on each shoulder. It was like sitting on top of a mountain. There were even little white flakes on the summit. His voice was so deep that only a highly trained ear or certain type of marine life could hear it. And when he entered a room, it stayed entered. From my first memory of him to the day he died (Death, too fearful of a frontal assault blind-sided him and he succumbed to cancer in his sixty-fourth year) I felt like an insignificant worm in his presence.

For all his manliness, though, Big Tom held some strange notions—including the belief that the Salvation Army was evil. It could have been something to do with their wearing black, I suppose, (though from what I remember, everyone in Maltby wore either grey or black, depending on the colour of the sky). But how he made the connection between the tambourine and the devil I will never know. When my mother was about ten he'd dragged her kicking and screaming out of a Salvation Army hymn session in which they had graciously allowed her to sing and play along. Although I'm not a huge fan of percussion music, it's hard for me to associate the tambourine with acts of wanton depravity. So, while I truly loved my grandad, if *I* was lying injured on the side of the road and given the choice of being nursed by the Sallies or an enormous Irish miner with a strange notion of the occult, I might just be persuaded to endure a bit of *rat-tat-tatting*.

Grandma, though no shrinking violet herself, was to me absolute kindness. Whenever I couldn't get Big Tom's attention or approval, or had been beaten by Trish for no other reason than daring to exist, I could always find safety in her cuddles and solace in her 'What's-the-matter-then?'.

The things I associate most with my grandma from this time are tea, scones, floral dresses and rodeos. Anyone who has known an elderly English lady will be familiar with their habit of sitting around drinking tea and scoffing scones in the sort of dress that looks like it could give you severe hay fever. But you don't mess with these women—they can wield a rolling pin like Bruce Lee brandishes a set of nunchukas. During the war-rationing years I can imagine a bunch of floral-clad pensioners stalking the alleys around tea-rooms and bingo halls, whispering to men in dark coats, 'C'mon, baby I'm hurting. Just a half-tin of Earl Grey and a quarter lemon and I'll see you right.'

The rodeos may come as a bit of a surprise, though, given the distance of Maltby from, say, Texas. My grandma's favourite teacup was not made of bone china—like the ones with the hand-painted periwinkles that most Yorkshire people would love to smash over Mrs Bucket's pretentious head. It was a light brown plastic number with a picture of a highly skilled and buttock-clenching cowboy on a bucking bronco. I think both the cowboy's hands were in the air, so how he managed to stay on board I can't imagine. I was never able to locate an obvious anchor point and I hope to God it wasn't what I thought it might be. Though that could explain the bronco's eagerness to dislodge him.

If Grandad and Grandma Kennedy were no-nonsense sort of people it was probably because Maltby was a no-nonsense sort of town. A spade was a bloody spade and that was the end of the matter, you bloody skirt-wearing wassack.

Lone dogs roamed the streets like tumbleweed on a mission. When you crossed the road you looked right, looked left, looked dog, as there was generally a hyena salivating close by, eager to separate flesh from limb.

And it was not uncommon to walk down the street and find yourself suddenly hit by an elderly lady six foot off the ground, arms and legs akimbo, her body parallel to the horizon. You immediately knew that she'd stepped where she shouldn't have and that the dog probably needed a bit more fibre in its diet.

Maybe it was the dampness, but the children of Maltby always appeared to be repulsively ill. Congealed stalactites hung from noses. The cold Yorkshire air slowed the dripping so that their removal no longer involved handkerchiefs, but scissors. Snail trails ran along jumper-sleeves and invited comparisons of length, width and texture.

For all its damp and dirt, though, Maltby was not without its admirers. Golden cornfields rippled at its edges: the drab picture almost turned into a work of art by its frame.

Maltby was, and still is, a working class town peopled mainly by miners, quarry men, brickyard workers and their families. There was always a feeling of struggle in the air, along with the smell of coal dust—which I suppose was good for the local economy, if not the lungs. It was a town that I, sickly little thing that I was, felt out of place in. Mum, Trish and I would wait at the bus stop only to have some miner standing next to us cough up half a lung and then casually say that it was a nice day for it. These men could spit like emphysemic camels and it impressed me almost as much as it repulsed Mum. Starting deep within the abdomen, they would build up pressure and froth before commencing the Newton-defying journey north. Tar-stained mucus would be collected on the way up, the chunky liquid giving their vocal cords a rattle on the way past and adding to the disturbing sound of the still churning stomach. Then there would be a hiatus between the final gargle and the heavy blatter of liquid hitting pavement, road, or, if we were lucky, handkerchief (or unlucky if you happened to be responsible for the guy's laundry).

Existing on a diet of Woodbines, alcohol and sandwiches lubricated with dripping, these were not men who worried too much about cholesterol levels or retirement plans. I wanted so desperately to be like them, but my own spitting technique, which involved placing my tongue between my lips and blowing an insipid raspberry, needed some serious work before I would be sprinkled with coal dust and admitted to their ranks. At three years old, though, the die was already cast and I knew I was too much of a mummy's boy to aspire to being one of the bus stop spitters. Unknown to me, Mum had seen her father and two brothers "go down t'pit", and was formulating a plan to ensure that I, and my soon-to-arrive brother Paul, wouldn't have to follow them.

Times were not easy and people did what they could to make ends meet. One house in the street sold toffee apples while another sold eggs and, somewhere in between, another woman sold her body. Or at least that's what the older boys in the street said. I tried to imagine her offering an arm or leg up for sale, but I couldn't. It seemed such an absurd notion. I wondered what people would do with her body and stretched my mind almost until it broke.

3

Working Class Car Wash

The most thrilling ride on the planet was to sit in the front seat upstairs in a double-decker bus as it veered and lurched down winding country lanes while Death sat there quietly, already banished by my mother to the back row.

The driver, safely separated from the rest of us in his own little compartment, clearly didn't care much about passenger safety or local ecology as he tore through the tops of hedgerows and the lower branches of trees. This was the working class kids' car wash and I loved every minute of it.

Just when it seemed that the driver could take a sweeping curve no faster, he suddenly adopted a *you-ain't-seen-nothing-yet!* approach and actually accelerated into the curve. This left all the adults biting their knuckles and all the boys jumping up and down and vowing to become bus drivers when they grew up. Such a trip always made me fiercely proud because my dad was a bus driver, though I can't actually remember being on a bus when he was at the wheel. Maybe it was some sort of family thing, like surgeons not being allowed to operate on their relatives—much as they might like to. Perhaps the Rotherham Bus Company deemed it unsafe for a driver to try and concentrate on the road while his wife sat behind, reminding him constantly that he was a complete pillock.

The only time I felt scared was whenever another bus loomed up at us menacingly out of the fog. Miraculously we would somehow always avoid impact, though there could never have been more than a cigarette paper between the two buses. And you knew this because the drivers often exchanged cigarettes, matches or nods as they passed.

4

The Beast in the Bramble Patch

Maltby had a fairly large Catholic congregation, no doubt swollen by the influx of Irish labour in the fifties. The priest, the aptly named Father Coleman, was a kind-hearted old fellow who would regularly visit his parishioners with words of wisdom, comfort and hope for a better life, if not in this one then the one hereafter. In return he would receive tea, biscuits and I suppose occasional offers of sex—depending on the house he happened to be visiting, the mood of its occupant and how far they had strayed from the path of the big shepherd.

At our house it was strictly tea and biscuits. My parents, hard-working, clean-living, church-going folk, who I'm sure were forced to invent sins so that they could attend confession, did not need spiritual or moral guidance. Father Coleman's visits to our house would have been for refreshment purposes only, after he had

knocked on most of the troubled doors in the street—
including that of the lady whose house sat somewhere
between the ones that sold eggs and toffee apples.

Although he was a regular visitor to our street, the
only time I can actually remember for myself Father
Coleman calling on us was when Trish had just tried to
sever my spinal column with a fork.

I was sitting on the back steps rubbing my wound
and my eyes and sniffling the sniffle of the hard-done-
by, while Mum prodded the bramble patch with her
specially sharpened broom handle. She looked like one
of those sadistic magicians who lock their bikinied assis-
tants in a box and then proceed to dismember them
with swords because they've asked for a pay rise. I'd
never actually seen a magician take a run-up, though,
or utter the words, "swine", "bloody" and "little" with
such venom. But who knows what the tv producers cut
from their variety programs before they go to air?

I had just about regained the use of my legs when
there was an apparition in black before me. I gasped.
Death had returned while Mum was busy skewering the
bramble patch.

'What seems to be the matter, young man?' the old
priest said.

'Trish stabbed me.'

'Trish stabbed me, *Father*.'

I couldn't work out why he would say such an odd
thing. I didn't know that priests had fathers, and even
if they had, I doubted that Trish would be on such

familiar terms with Father Coleman's father as to lurch at him with a knife.

'Trish stabbed me *father*?'

'That's better. And where's Trish now?'

'Down't back in t'bush. Mum's guin to bloody murder her.' I pointed to the back corner of the garden where Mum was spearfishing.

'I'll bloody murder you, you little swine! Just wait till I get my hands on you! Get yourself out here this bloody instant!' Even though I was only three, I didn't think that this would tempt Trish out.

'Now, now, Mrs Larkin.'

'Bugger off!' yelled Mum, obviously under the impression that she was being counselled by the postman.

'Now, *now*, Mrs Larkin,' admonished Father Coleman. 'There's no call for *that*.'

Mum turned around with a look that I thought would be followed by the launch of her broom. As soon as she saw it was Father Coleman, though, she was absolutely mortified. She apologised so profusely that you would have thought she was assuming responsibility for Protestantism. No penance would have been too great—even self-immolation, if Father Coleman had imposed it and happened to have a match on him.

As Mum ushered him inside with even greater apologies and offers of tea, biscuits—and that was absolutely all—with stinging eyes I glanced up at the bramble patch. It started to giggle.

5

The Seaside

Across the road from us lived the Loaders. Knowing that I'd been ill with just about everything—meningitis, gastroenteritis, older-sisteritis—Margaret Loader ran into Mum in the street and asked after my health. The terse, 'He's fine thank you,' translated, 'Sod off, nosy cow!' Margaret, however, had lived through the war and was not about to be verbally strafed off her own street. And, seeing someone who was doing it fairly tough, she continued to hold out the hand of friendship until it was accepted.

The Loaders became our best and dearest friends and remain so despite, and perhaps due to, practically thirty years living apart from us.

Margaret's husband Harry is unique. He has to be the only man in history who has ever admitted to being a spectacularly bad driver. He has plenty of evidence to support his claim, though. Once in the middle of winter, he drove into an enormous seaside car park where there was only one other car that was parked a couple of hundred metres away. Somehow he managed to hit it.

Margaret and Harry had three children: Hazel who was studying to become a teacher; Keith, a mad keen Rotherham United supporter and possibly the funniest person on the planet; and Catherine who was the same age as Trish, though not nearly half as psychotic.

On rainy days when we couldn't go out, Trish and Catherine would hold me down and tickle my feet until I was fit to vomit.

We soon discovered that what the Loaders loved most of all was going on trips to "the seaside". We hadn't realised it because we didn't own a car, but this was some sort of national disease. The sky can be black and dripping blood, the Four Horsemen of the Apocalypse have just hoven into view, and English people will still pack their cars with knee-rugs, windbreaks, jumpers, anoraks, blankets and steaming flasks, and drive to "the seaside". They spend hours huddled near or in their cars, wearing coats that make them look like nylon sheep and saying improbable things like, 'Eee, isn't this grand', or 'We must do this again', or the certifiable, 'You can keep your Costa Brava. Give me Skegness and a flask of tea any day of the week'.

On one trip to Skegness (or "Skegsnest" as I called it), Trish, Catherine Loader and I were in the back of the Loaders' Austin 1100 when Harry announced that he could see the sea, although we were still many miles from the coast.

Trish chimed in, saying that she could see it too; and although there was nothing but houses and hills in every direction, I said that I could see it as well, in case Trish suddenly reached across and clawed me to death for contradicting her. Catherine, however, looked all around us for the seaside but it was nowhere to be seen.

'Look,' said Harry, 'there's a boat.'

'Yes,' exclaimed Trish.

'Er, yes,' I said.

'Where?' said Catherine.

'And there's a man fishing on the boat.' Harry had struck a rich seam of bullshit and was keen to see how deep it ran.

'Oh yes,' said Trish.

'Mmnn,' I said.

'*Where?*' spat Catherine, her bottom lip starting to quiver.

'And look,' said Margaret, joining in the fun, 'he's caught a little fish.'

'Oh he has,' said Harry.

'Oh he has too!' yelped Trish.

'Mn,' was all I could manage.

'*WHERE?*'

Margaret and Harry spent the rest of the journey in hysterics. This didn't at all aid Harry's skill behind the wheel. Meanwhile Catherine lapsed into a permanent sulk, her face only brightened by the fluorescent glow of her orange cardigan.

6

Going to School with Bill and Ben

Almost before it had begun, toddlerhood was over and infancy began in earnest. There was a definite cut-off date: the day I started school.

What changed my life wasn't exactly the Victorian rule of sadistic schoolmasters who would, according to Yorkshire folklore at least, beat you limbless for so much as touching a pencil with your left hand. In fact the most taxing problem we encountered during our first year at school was being asked to join the dots in a vague numerical sequence. Mum has always claimed that when she was at school in Thryberg she was thrashed senseless every day—even if she hadn't done anything wrong. According to her, the headmaster lined up against the wall those children who hadn't done any-thing thrashable and soundly beat them to within an inch of their lives, to warn them what *would* happen if they *did* do anything thrashable the next day.

After this merciless clouting, she would have to carry her three siblings, Tom, Tim and Cathleen, home on her back, barefoot over broken glass, through mine fields, driving snow and across the great Doncaster and Barnsley glacier. And when she got them home she would be forced to run odd jobs for her neighbour, Mrs Wassack, who would beat her half to death with a rolling pin wrapped in barbed wire for daring to look at her sideways.

I didn't dread my very first day at school as I was to dread later first days. There was no nervous build-up from weeks of having to try on uniforms or stiff school shoes with the lion paw-prints on the sole and compass in the heel. There were no uniforms at Maltby Catholic School, so we dressed as we did normally, which in Yorkshire—even in summer—made us look like hypothermic bears. Mum is one of those people who believe that it always gets cold later on, so she dressed us accordingly. I could be on the first manned space flight to Venus and she would be there at the launch site, reminding me to take a jumper.

'But, Mum, it's over seven hundred degrees on Venus.'

'Yes,' she would reply, 'but it gets nippy in the afternoons.'

I would be strolling around the Venusian surface in my ten-million-dollar NASA climate-controlled space-suit, with an enormous orange cardigan over it. 'That's one small step for man; one great big cardy from the Pat Larkin casual knitwear range.'

It's strange that, although I had about as much self-confidence as a caffeine-addicted chihuahua, the thought of going to school didn't bother me. My cousin Jacqueline was going to be in the same class. So was my friend Shaun from across the road. (He lived next door to the people with the circular window). Trish and Catherine Loader were a couple of years ahead, and seeing Trish's face in the corridors was actually quite comforting—even if it was fixed in an almost perma-nent maniacal leer. All things considered, I was rather looking forward to school.

The only thing we had to do on our first day was give our names and watch *Bill and Ben the Flowerpot Men, Andy Pandy* and *The Magic Roundabout* which, though confusing, was not exactly taxing as there was no written exam to follow.

At the age I was, of course, I didn't know a great deal about hallucinogenic drugs in the sixties, but it's hard to imagine these shows being created without the assistance of some seriously high-grade shit. The writ-ers of *Bill and Ben* obviously had the same dealer as those from *The Magic Roundabout*. It's the only way I can explain what was happening on the screen. The opening scene from the pilot script of *Bill and Ben* must have gone something like this:

1. Ext. Farm. Day.

Two Flower Pots (Bill and Ben) are standing next to a weed (Weed) of indeterminate origin.

Bill

Flobadob, flobadod, flobadob, dob dob, Weed.

Ben

Flobadob, flobadod, flobadob, dob dob, little Weed.

Weed

Weeeeeeed.

And yet the project was given the green light. Weird.

The creators of *The Magic Roundabout* must have got hold of some advance psycho-technology and had somehow managed to download the contents of Jimi Hendrix's mind after an eventful Saturday night out with, say, Keith Richards.

Andy Pandy confused us for no other reason than that we never could determine his or her sex. This was important because if you were going to nickname somebody "Andy Pandy" at a later date, you had to be sure of your ground.

Andy Pandy him/herself seemed to spend a lot of time in his/her picnic hamper, washing basket, or whatever the hell it was. Perhaps he/she was trying to come to grips with the question that had the rest of us stumped and required hours of blackened privacy to achieve it.

The only thing I learned in my first couple of weeks at school was that there were some kids who didn't want to be there. They would be dragged into class, clinging to their mothers with a grip like an electrocuted cat. Only the trained eye of the teacher could tell where parent ended and child began. They would screech about having to be there until eventually the school janitor was summoned and he would prise them loose with his shovel.

Our teacher, Mrs Walsh, was always wonderfully calming and conciliatory in these situations and projected a confident air to the parents that was obviously an integral part of the training at teachers' college. However as soon as the parent had left, the child would be inserted into its seat, where it could put its head down and whimper and heave those convulsive sobs all it liked. If its head hadn't surfaced again by play lunch, Mrs Walsh could be relied on to start firing bits of chalk at it, while the tough kids behind would reach forward and push its chair legs with their feet.

I was a long way from being one of the tough kids, but I wasn't one of the electrocuted cats either. Caught somewhere in the middle of no-man's-land, I would alternate between feeling sorry for the poor little thing who had been abandoned yet again, and reaching forward to push its chair with my feet.

I was four. I was fickle. Sue me.

7

Cry Baby

I only ever cried once in class and that was in my second
year. Sammy Thornton, who was sitting in the seat in
front of me, fell forward onto his desk with his hands
buried in his arms and started bawling. I was just about
to reach forward and push his chair with my feet when
the smell cannoned up my nasal passages and bounced
off the back of my skull like a startled goat. That smell
was not of this earth. The school nurse and her hose
were going to be no help at all on this one. Nothing
less than a priest with a mantra would do.

Pugsley Porksworth was the official classroom shitter. Apart from the problems with his internal plumbing,
he seemed to have a note that excluded him from, or
permitted him to do, just about anything—and that
included crapping anywhere he pleased.

But Pugsley Porksworth was absent on this particular day, possibly with a severe bout of dysentery.

So unless this reek was wafting over from his house (not impossible) someone else was to blame.

Half the members of our class were immediately absolved because they were girls. I didn't exactly see them swinging from higher branches on the evolutionary tree than the rest of us, but I simply couldn't imagine a girl doing such a thing. I blocked the idea out. And if it hadn't been for Trish regularly and spitefully pissing on my toys, I would have sworn that they didn't go to the toilet at all.

In no time Mrs Walsh's nose started to quiver like a hungry rat's. 'Does somebody need to use the bathroom?' she said.

'I think somebody already has, Miss.'

'Thank you, Mark Little.'

'It was John Larkin, Miss.'

'It was not!'

'Be quiet, the both of you!'

'Then why do you look like you're going to cry, Larkin?'

I collapsed onto my desk, head buried in my arms, and started to snivel.

Mrs Walsh went on a short sniffing expedition that centred on me.

'Could you go and get the nurse please, Jacqueline?' she said.

From my buried position I could hear my cousin's feet padding down the hall outside towards the administration area. The rest of the class was busy opening windows and in no time about thirty or so heads were stuck out in the rain.

Jacqueline returned with the nurse and the remainder of the class were ordered back to their seats, most of them begging to be allowed to stay by the window a bit longer.

'Come with me, please,' said a stern voice, clearly not relishing what lay ahead.

I summoned what little courage I had left and sat up—not an easy task when your chair is constantly being pushed from behind.

'What's the matter with *you*, John?' asked Mrs Walsh.

Sammy Thornton's head and, more crucially, his trousers, disappeared around the open door with the vexed school nurse, who wasn't a nurse at all, merely an administrative assistant with nursing aspirations.

'It was the smell, Miss. It made me feel sick.'

'That's okay. Would you like to go outside for some air?'

'Yes, please.'

I stood up, walked outside to my peg and put on my coat and checked cap with the woollen flaps for the ears, leaving behind—along with the smell—cries of:

'That's not fair, Miss.'

'I feel sick too, Miss.'

'I think I'm gunna cry, Miss.'

Ignoring the rain, I walked outside, down the back

of the schoolyard and decided to go after a few earwigs, which lived in holes on the wooden fence.

Poor Sammy Thornton. I would almost have felt sorry for him if I hadn't been so busy feeling miserable for myself. It was my birthday party at the weekend and Sammy was one of the few kids from school whom I had invited. And now everyone would know that *I* was friends with a classroom shitter. What little playground cred I'd built up over the last two years had come crashing down around me in one fell poop.

8

Pigs in Waistcoats and Top Hats

It seems almost fateful that men who spent the week under the earth's surface, mining the very soil on which they lived, spent so much of their own time on weekends cultivating it.

My granddad, Big Tom, was a proud man with a fierce sense of what was right and his allotment gave him the chance to put back into the earth what he'd taken out of it. I always felt that there was a certain amount of poetry in this, though mercifully I kept these thoughts to myself and avoided copping a clout for being so bloody daft.

Either Big Tom's impressive farming skills were innate or he had picked them up in Sligo. Like him, many miners had had a rural upbringing. They might have had coal dust in their lungs, but farming was in their blood. At the sound of the Industrial Revolution, however, they had come in from the fields like Eloi to join the Morloch under the earth.

Apart from vegetables, Big Tom used his allotment for chickens, which he kept for eggs, cows, which he kept for milk, and pigs, which he would dress up in waistcoats and top hats for his private amusement. Or at least that's what I imagined—not being too sure what purpose the pigs served. I'd never connected them with bacon or black pudding.

But for all his toughness, Big Tom was a cat man. He couldn't walk anywhere on his allotment without having a dozen or so of them winding in and out of his legs. When it was feeding time there were so many tails in the air that they looked like the dodgem cars at Morecambe fun fair. When he was dozing by the fire at home with a book in one hand and his pipe in the other, there was so much purring around his lap that you would have sworn he had a helicopter tucked away in his trousers.

Whenever he stumbled over one of his multitude of moggies, rather than smite it dead, he would pick himself up and ask after its health with a warm, 'Are you all right, then?' I had a fair idea that if he'd ever tripped over my scrawny body it might have been a different story. I suppose given the number of rats in Maltby, the moggies did have a purpose. I was a long way from discovering mine.

9

Dr Who and the Attack of the Adenoids

Around the time the word "Australia" was being bandied about our house, I started to lose my hearing. I can't remember actually going deaf, but I was certainly heading that way when Mum took me to see an ear, nose and throat specialist in Rotherham.

I knew that I didn't hear too well because Big Tom had nicknamed me "You Wot". Every time he asked me a question or gave me a command, I would look at him quizzically and say 'You what?'.

Mum was much more worried about my hearing than I was. I was quite happy to cocoon myself off in my own little world, but she was desperate to get out of Maltby and doubtless aware that having a deaf child would probably hinder our chances of being accepted by Australia House. The door was slamming shut on her escape plans and t'pit was beckoning Paul and me.

The doctor's office was bigger than our house: the expanse of his magnificent polished desk so large that he was forced to use a loud-hailer to talk to Mum. His car must have stretched into next week. Having made his way around from his side of the desk—a journey of just under two kilometres—he surveyed me over the top of his glasses in a way that had me wondering why he was wearing glasses at all if he didn't need them to see.

What was said in the consultation this particular day I don't remember—partly because the doctor had trekked the distance back to his side of the desk, but mostly because I was almost stone deaf. I think the gist of it, though, was that I had something wrong with my adenoids and that once they were removed I would regain my hearing.

Mum was so relieved that as soon as we were out of the surgery, she headed for the toy shop and bought me a five-hundred piece jigsaw puzzle.

When we arrived home Trish was still concerned that my adenoids would prevent us from going to Australia (whatever or wherever that was) and if they did, she promised to give me a good clout.

I sat on the ground doing my jigsaw puzzle without the faintest idea what adenoids were. They sounded like the sort of thing Dr Who would set about once he'd finished zapping the Daleks—but if having them out meant avoiding another clouting from Trish, then I was happy to see the back of them.

My uncle Tim was adamant that there was no such bloody thing as adenoids and that the bloody quack was only putting me in hospital so he could buy himself a bloody new yacht.

A few days later I was admitted to hospital, although given that my operation was performed under the NHS, it was probably *months*. There were seven other children in my ward, none of whom appeared to be even remotely ill. As soon as the nurse left the ward they would leap out of bed, batter each other around the head with their pillows, charge about playing cowboys and Indians, and generally beat the living daylights out of one another. Being the youngest by a good few years, I hung back from the physical stuff and was content to shoot passers-by from the safety of my bed.

The following day I was wheeled along the corridor and into the operating theatre backwards, which was really disorientating. As were the multitude of surgical-masked faces that loomed over me. I still didn't have any idea what adenoids were, but their removal was obviously a big job, judging by the number of doctors and nurses involved.

Eventually Donald Duck and Mickey Mouse eased me off the trolley and onto the operating table, where Goofy immediately slapped the back of my hand and shoved a needle in it. I suppose the masks were to make children feel at ease. Unfortunately, however, the Disney Corporation had not yet penetrated Yorkshire as far as

Maltby, and I drifted off to sleep convinced that my adenoids were about to be torn violently out of wherever they were by a rat, a bird, and a rather unconvincing dog in a silly hat.

10

The Curse of the Headless Ted

For my fifth birthday I was given a teddy bear. I haven't a clue why I called him Michael rather than, say, Ted or Mr Bear. Perhaps there was a famous Michael gadding about England in the late sixties (Caine? Crawford?) who had influenced me.

Michael's arrival in the family, however, soon pushed Trish over the edge. Or maybe I'd got her hackles up by breathing through my mouth again—which people with a permanently blocked nose do. Or perhaps my blond hair had reflected the sun into her eyes and annoyed her. Or maybe it was my having the audacity to celebrate my birthday in April while hers wasn't until July. Who knows why, but my darling sister had decided that Michael's special swivel head was coming off.

I don't know how she did it, but when on the following evening I picked up Michael to take him outside for a game of football, he immediately did his Marie Antoinette impersonation. I stared at the floor in horror as his head rolled towards the fireplace. It looked, for one terrifying moment, as if it was going to roll all the way into the flames. But my five-year-old mind had failed to factor in the dramatic deceleration effect of the average teddy bear's snout and it stopped short. I didn't know a whole lot about physics in the sixties, but I knew a thing or two about sisters and I was already working on a theory.

Mum had watched the entire floor show in stunned disbelief from her place on the settee. I was sure I could hear a sharp intake of breath coming from somewhere behind Dad's armchair, which, had I not been preoccupied, I would have sworn was a snigger.

I felt it first through the soles of my feet: a distant rumble that originated in the bowels of the earth. It was a sound that might, on a long cold night, be followed by the lone howl of a dog, and have you wondering whether your "Home and Contents" insurance policy covers earthquakes. The rumble carried on up my shins, through my knees and made them knock uncontrollably. It picked up force and resonance at my groin and pushed my testicles back up into my body, when they'd only just come down. Abandoning my still retreating young gonads, it arrived at my empty stomach, (we hadn't had dinner yet). It crashed painfully over each rib like a surfboat through the breakers. It careered on up my throat, gave my vocal cords a rattle and produced an involuntary high-pitched scream. Finally it clattered along my jawbone and screeched out of my ears. **'TRISH! GET BLOODY IN HERE THIS INSTANT!'**

The slam of the back door and Trish's hysterical shrieking as she leapt headfirst into the bramble patch meant that Mum would have to bloody well see to her later.

With a sneer in the direction of the bramble patch, Mum hopped into action. She said there was some wool in her sewing kit specially for reattaching the heads of bears that had been removed by *'bloody little vixens!'* She picked up both parts of Michael and bounded up the stairs two at a time—the eighth step almost shattering on impact—and not twenty minutes later, Michael was almost as good as new. Granted he would never be able to swivel his head again, but to be honest I'd always thought this was a bit of a gimmick, and was never sure why a teddy bear needed 360-degree vision anyway—except for perhaps keeping an eye on Trish.

'What do you think?' said Mum, holding up Michael.

'What's that bright stuff round his neck?'

'It's my special bear-mending wool. Bears like orange. It's their favourite colour. Besides, it looks like he's got his own little scarf. All your friends will be jealous.' Such was Mum's power over me that we could have been hanging off the stern of the *Titanic*, as it made its final desperate plunge, and she could have said, 'It'll be okay, lovey. Captain's just gone to get the rest of the lifeboats. He'll be back in a tick.' And I would have believed her and gone off to sleep.

The wool looked suspiciously like a bit left over from the matching cardigans that Mum had knitted for Trish and Catherine Loader: the ones with the big buttons that I both loved and hated. "Loved" because Trish hated wearing it due to her strange phobia of buttons. (Her other phobias were tea and margarine. If there are any child psychologists tuning in, then I'm afraid you'll just have to take a ticket and wait. Years later I would exact revenge by regularly offering Trish cups of tea with huge dobs of margarine and buttons floating on top). "Hated" because she would vent her orange-cardigan-wearing rage on me.

But Mum had said that it was special teddy bear-mending wool and that was the end of the matter. I thought it was hilarious that Trish and Catherine (who has also developed a significant fear of buttons) didn't have a clue that their fluorescent cardigans were not made from proper wool at all, but from the stuff that was set aside to mend teddy bears.

If I have portrayed my sister as the devil incarnate, I've been unfair to devils. Like Mum, Trish had a strong nursing instinct and liked nothing better than to soothe my brow and hush my sobs whenever I'd hurt myself or when things just became too much for me.

Unfortunately, being the impatient sort, she was not about to hang around until I found something to be injured by or to sob over. So she would regularly hurl me down the steps, run at me with her bike and set about me with the contents of the cutlery drawer or Mum's sewing kit, until I'd reached a state requiring a nurse or an ambulance.

Because we lived in a three-bedroom house, both Trish and I had our own rooms. I thought this was heaven because even as a toddler I craved personal space—as would anyone with an older sister like her. The nights passed so peacefully that even now I can see squirrels, doves and angels at my bedroom window, ushering me safely through the dark hours while the beast lurked right next door.

Whenever Trish had a nightmare, or was scared of the dark, storms or margarine and giant tea-soaked buttons, or whenever my adenoids were keeping her up again, she would bustle into my room, wake me up and impatiently tell me that I was having a nightmare and that I'd better sleep with her so that she could look after me. I would gather up Michael and crawl gratefully into her double bed, never once pausing to wonder why I was unable to remember my nightmare.

One morning I woke to discover that Michael had wet the bed. His fur was damp, matted and on closer inspection had a musty, sickly odour wafting from it. When the poor thing was decapitated he had obviously suffered permanent brain damage and total loss of bladder control. I started snivelling.

'What's wrong with *you*?'

'Michael wet the bed.'

'Don't be stupid. Teddy bears—even the ones with dumb names—can't wet the bed.'

'Feel him.'

Trish ran her hand down to where bears would urinate from if they could.

'Err, yuck!'

'See.'

'It wasn't him; it was *you*. You're disgusting! **MUM, JOHN WET MY BED!** You're dead.'

I could almost hear the static electricity being generated as Mum threw on her nightgown. This was followed by the deafening clomp of slipper on floor that drowned out the thump of my heart.

'What's going on in here, you pair?'

'He wet the bed, Mum.'

'I'm sorry,' I quivered.

'That's okay, lovey. Accidents happen.'

'Get him out of here! The dirty little thing.'

'I wet Michael tooooooooo.'

'Don't cry,' said Mum. 'I'll hang him out on the line to dry. He'll be as right as rain. Bears like hanging on the line by their ears. It's their favourite thing.'

Mum ruffled my hair and pulled back the bedclothes.

'We'll soon have you cleaned up.' She felt my pyjamas. 'You *haven't* wet the bed.'

'I have. Feel Michael.'

She felt Michael's groin. I'm not sure why she did this because I'm certain by this point she would have had her own suspicions that had nothing to do with an incontinent teddy bear. She reached across Michael and felt Trish's nightdress. 'It's *you*, you bloody thing!'

Trish leapt out of bed like a demented frog, laughing wildly.

'Fancy blaming him. Come back here, you little swine!'

But it was too late. She was gone. Not even the eighth step dared impede her flight.

II

The Baths

Rare though it was, in summer the mercury could go over ninety. When this happened, Maltby, much more familiar with snow and driving rain, became Meltby. When the temperature gauge hit seventy, bald men suddenly found it necessary to wear handkerchiefs on their heads and "Kiss me Quick" t-shirts. At eighty, these same men would have to be physically restrained from hosing down passers-by in the name of community spirit.

Wilting in a deckchair on the back lawn, Mum would cast visual daggers at the sky in a futile search for an orbiting NASA satellite to blame the unseasonable heat on, before telling us to go and change for "t'baths".

We would arrive at Maltby Baths with arms full of rubber rings, inflatable life preservers, a load of foam, and our coats and cardigans because it was bound to get nippy later on. We would bob around the shallow end, buoyed up by enough inflatable material to raise the *Titanic*.

John Larkin

Building an outdoor pool in northern England makes about as much sense as a haemophiliac taking up knife juggling, and the baths have long since been reduced to rubble and its former site reclaimed by the earth.

In a millennium or two, archaeologists will use little brushes to whisk away the centuries of accumulated muck and wonder what sort of primeval rituals occurred at this ancient aquatic site. And if by chance one of their number suggests belly-busters, bombs, jack-knives and pissing in the shallow end, then this will be referred to as a successful dig.

12

My Dad the Arms Smuggler

Not long before we emigrated to Australia, Dad had to return to Ireland because his mother was ill. Perhaps tired of my incessant questions, Mum told me that Grandma Larkin had a loose head and I immediately wondered if Trish had been up to her old tricks. In any event, Dad had to go home to see if he could help put things right.

I wandered around for days, wondering what sort of accident could have caused my poor grandma's head to come loose. I even walked around wobbling my own to try and see what living with a loose head would be like. Something as relatively simple as chasing sparrows up the hill in our back lawn, my head wobbling with each step, caused me to fall over, and I hoped that Grandma Larkin's back lawn didn't have a hill and that if it did she saw no reason to chase birds up it. Kicking a football in the air was next to impossible when you had a head like one of those nodding dogs that sat on the rear windows of cars in the sixties and seventies for no clear reason. But I was fairly sure that Grandma Larkin's football days were long behind her, even though I had met her just once and couldn't remember much about her daily habits. The only thing I was sure of was that Irish grandmothers, or all grandmothers, went in for a lot of praying. I walked into the lounge room and knelt beneath a picture of Jesus with my head bouncing as if it was on a spring and felt happy that having a loose head didn't interfere with your prayers. In fact it probably improved them. Nodding along, it looked as though you were agreeing with God.

Even so, I was still worried that Grandma's loose head might actually come away and that maybe Mum ought to have gone with Dad and taken her bear-mending wool with her.

When Dad arrived home, about a week or so later, I asked him how Grandma's head was—and, more to the point, *where* it was. He gave me the sort of look that I imagine he normally kept for the English or for people from County Kerry. Then he went upstairs, unpacked his suitcase and brought me down a plastic tommy-gun that he'd picked up in Dublin. (It's just occurred to me that you would have to have been a foolhardy Irishman indeed to pass through an English port carrying a machine-gun, plastic or otherwise! I don't think that this was a gift that he'd fully thought through—understandably, I suppose, given the unstable state of his mother's head).

13

The Olympics, the Lollipop Man and the Cock

There was only one class for each of the years from 1 to 6 at Maltby Catholic School, which suggests that the community wasn't nearly as pious as I'd believed.

The main building was a long thin affair with a corridor running its full length and the rooms off to one side of it. You started at one end of the building and worked your way through the years until you emerged at the other—punctuated with a spell in The Portable somewhere around year 4—ready for either the local comprehensive or grammar schools. A games-room-cum-dinner-hall was at the centre of the building and that was as far as I ever dared journey. Beyond, there was a cock and a cock aspirant in the senior years who would think nothing of flushing your head down the toilet or making you walk through the trough in nothing but your socks. Or force you at gunpoint to eat dog-shit sandwiches. Or sell you to gypsies for fag money. Or murder you in cold blood and dance naked on your grave in protest at the quality of school lunches.

For some reason the toughest kid in sixth grade was called the cock. He wasn't necessarily the school bully, but rather the kid who was generally regarded as the best fighter. And indeed the cock would often sort out the bully when either the bully had overstepped the mark or the cock needed to enhance a flagging reputation.

I don't know how the cock earned his position, as I cannot remember a single fight at the school in the two and a half years I was there. I suppose a pecking order was established as you moved up through the school. Then on the final day of term, when the old cock was about to leave the school and you were the fifth grade cock, you were officially the cock-elect.

I don't think any formal ceremony actually took place for the cock hand-over, but everybody knew who the cock was and the likes of me weren't deemed worthy enough of looking the cock in the eye. (If you are reading a subtext in any of this, wipe that smirk off your face, go out and rent a Dick Emery video and come back when you've got things straight in your mind!) One of my greatest thrills from that time was seeing the cock-elect down at the shops one weekend—the *weekend,* no less. I could hardly wait to get back to school with my news.

On Blyth Road, opposite the Crags, was Maltby Protestant School. Naturally all the students who attended this evil institution were damned to an eternity of wailing and gnashing of teeth in the fire pits of hell, which was a bit of a shame really, because they just seemed like ordinary kids to me.

Occasionally the two schools would meet in a sort of Crusade-with-schoolbags. We were going to pound fifteen types of tripe out of them because our god was right and theirs had mucked it up completely, while they were all going to jump on our heads until we came to our senses and followed their shepherd into the field of light.

Most of the time we were all just a happy babble of children streaming home, irrespective of our inherited denominations. But then somebody would get his back up about something on tv and suddenly we all became IRA recruits, intent on smashing the state from within, whereas up to that point we'd only been discussing what type of gobstopper we were planning to buy at the Globe supermarket.

The Protestant kids would come tearing down the hill from the Crags to meet us on our way up Muglet Lane. The idea was that their cock would meet our cock to see who had the best cock I suppose. At least that was the plan. When there were a hundred or so

Protestant kids baying for Catholic blood and vice versa (although this was England, sectarianism drifted across the Irish sea—both ways), a one-on-one wasn't going to cut it and you had to weigh into the melee yourself if you were positioning yourself as a future cock.

The thing was, nothing really ever came of these meetings apart from a bit of push and shove. They were usually broken up by the Lollipop Man before they had a chance to escalate.

The presence of the Lollipop Man was essential for those who, like me, were too young to enter into the fray and had to be content to hang around the edges, desperate to witness a bit of action. You always knew where the centre of the trouble was by his bright orange and yellow lollipop-stick, bobbing and swaying above the crowd with the ebb and flow of the shove.

Most of the time, the Lollipop Man was an impressive negotiator. Dispersing a couple of hundred revved-up kids with one hand—while the other hung onto his lollipop-stick—was no mean feat. Whatever gift of the gab and diplomacy he had, however, had usually deserted him by the time he got through to the back of the crowd. All he ever managed to bestow on us was a breathless, 'Bugger off, or I'll give you a thick ear!'

Often, Trish would have dragged me away before he got there. Not so much due to her instinctive sisterly duty of care, but because she considered me her private property and if anyone was going to give me a thorough clouting, it would be her.

I realised pretty early in the piece that I was never going to be the cock of my year when it came our time to be seniors. How was I going to convince people that I was the cock of anything, when I was being thrashed daily by a girl with pigtails and a bright orange cardigan just two years ahead of us.

Mark Little, though, had other ideas. He came from a family who lived on the wrong side of the tracks, which, taking into account the backwoods howl of passing steam trains, could have been just about anywhere in Maltby. The Littles lived in the ironically named Model Village: a sort of hexagonal maze across the road from our school, which only a few brave souls dared enter, and from which only the strongest and most resolute returned. At night the wind carried the distant wail of wild dogs and the blood-curdling screams of unwary travellers who had been drawn into its labyrinth and carved up for conkers. At least that's what Trish would tell me after she had woken me up from one of my regular nightmares and ordered me to come and sleep under her protective eiderdown.

Sammy Thornton also lived in the Model Village, and yet despite being far from tough himself, he appeared to have worked out a rather effective defence strategy. Although clearly a burden on his family's laundry budget, the regular dumping in his pants obviously prevented his being either beaten or bitten, depending on the species or mood of his assailant.

Mark Little's brothers had been cocks of the school in their time, as had his father before them, so it was a heritage he rightly felt proud of. We all knew that Mark would be cock at the appropriate time, so he was clearly cock-in-waiting and the only positioning to be done was that of second cock-in-waiting; a slightly riskier endeavour than it would be today, given infant mortality rates in mining towns at the time.

For all his toughness Mark Little was not a bad kid by any stretch of the imagination. But he was big, fast and strong, so that much older boys stayed well out of his way. And yet he chose puny little me to be his friend. I was so shocked to be invited into his gang's exclusive ranks (it was a bit like Mr Bean being inducted into the Mafia) that I actually asked Mark if he was taking the piss. I'd overheard an older boy use that expression and had been dying to insert it into one of my own conversations. It wasn't, however, my language that had impressed Mark, but my sporting ability.

Mrs Walsh had obviously been inspired by the Mexico Olympics, because she unexpectedly decided to hold a mini athletic carnival for our class in the dinner-hall. Our only previous exposure to sport had been the utter anarchy of playground football, where you could undo a goal that had been scored against your team by kicking the (insert:

ball,

rock,

shoe,

lunch-box,

glove,

scarf,

hat)

back through your own goal while the other team tried to stop you—provided that they hadn't run off to set fire to the girls' skipping ropes while they were in mid-skip.

Now we were suddenly required to stand in an orderly line and patiently wait our turn to jump, climb, skip, hop, bend and clap (okay, it wasn't exactly the Olympics) in time with Mrs Walsh's whistle.

Finally at the end of the games, just before a couple of thousand doves were released and the Olympic flag was passed to West Germany, Mrs Walsh decided it was time for a bit of serious competition. She set up a series of witches' hats and laid bamboo sticks across them. We then had to pair off and race down to the far end of the hall, where the loser would have to sit down while the winner was sent back to wait for the next round.

My opponent in the first race was Pugsley Porksworth who, given his weight problem, didn't appear to pose much of a threat. Apart from shitting himself daily as a protest against the quality of school dinners, he seemed to live in a surreal world of his own.

Mrs Walsh's whistle shrilled around us and I exploded off the mark. Although competition from Pugsley was unlikely, I was taking no chances and tore down the hall like a hyperactive gazelle, clearing each hurdle as if it was nothing more than a join in the floorboards. By the time I had broken the imaginary tape at the other end of the hall, Pugsley was lying in a screaming heap on the floor. He had become tangled up in the second hurdle and was regretting his decision to run on polished floorboards in his socks.

I won my second race almost as easily and by the time I had finished my third, Pugsley was just crossing the line for his first. He sat down with the other eliminees with such a *whummph* that the extra baggage he was carrying in his pants immediately shot up around his ears.

Finally it was down to just two of us: Mark Little and me. Of course the intelligent thing to do would have been to let Mark win; curry favour as it were. But I was five years old and didn't know a whole lot about curry. What I did enjoy, though, was running fast.

The kitchen staff were already setting up the dinner tables, so we had to make it quick. Mrs Walsh's whistle shrilled for the final time and we tore off, while the rest of the class, Pugsley Porksworth aside, went ballistic cheering us on. About halfway down I was vaguely aware of Mark's presence next to me, but I gritted my teeth and headed for home, arriving there a clear winner. My cousin Jacqueline had encouraged the rest of the girls in the class to cheer for me, so that was all rather exciting. But my moment in the spotlight was ruined by Mrs Walsh exchanging words with Pugsley Porksworth. He had found a note in his pocket that apparently excused him from jumping over hurdles on polished wooden floors while wearing socks. Mrs Walsh said that it was a bit late for that now, because we had finished. But Pugsley, defiant to the last, said that we would see about that and stormed off, brandishing his note and threatening to shit on the headmaster in protest.

14

A Cock-in-waiting

At lunch time, after collecting my piece of charred animal, cabbage and dessert that defied description—it was possibly meant to be some sort of custard, since it was yellow—I went and sat with my mates. We were all pretty nerdy, though I was probably the nerdiest. I was only a pair of taped-up glasses and an unscheduled crap away from having to sit with Pugsley Porksworth, Sammy Thornton and the rest of the classroom shitters. So my victory in the hurdles had at least maintained my position within the group—tenuous though it was.

I was just deciding whether or not to eat my main meal and dessert separately or dispense with caution and mix the lot together, when I was summoned to Mark Little's table by a couple of his henchmen. Naturally, I thought I was going to be pounded to a pulp, but the henchmen told me to bring my dinner with me. I wasn't sure if I was being asked to join them or offer my dinner at Mark's feet, or whether they were going to hurl it at me.

'You can sit by me,' said Mark, nodding at the seat next to him, which was occupied. On his nod, though, everyone shuffled down one seat to make room for my bony little butt.

Mark oversaw proceedings like Augustus, though I doubt very much that the first Emperor of Rome would have had a snail trail running practically the length of his toga.

Had I been twenty years older, I like to think I would have said something like, 'Peel me a fucking grape' and returned to my real friends. But I was thrilled.

'You're a fast runner,' said Mark, chewing on a chunk of custard in an off-hand, sardonic sort of way—*I know I'm supposed to eat this custard or get into trouble, but I'm eating it because I choose to.* The subtle complexities of being a cock, or future cock, it dawned on me, were mind-boggling. Mark even reached across and ate the custard belonging to one of the other members of his gang, just to show that he could. I didn't know how to respond to his "fast runner" comment, but fortunately it appeared to be a statement rather than a question.

'I've got to go t'bog,' announced Mark a while later, as if this was of the remotest interest to anyone. However, the way the other gang members immediately sat up suggested that it was.

Mark cast a look round the table and it landed on me. 'You can come wi'me,' he said. Disappointment rippled down the table. Given the hangdog looks of the others, accompanying Mark to the toilet was clearly a significant part of cock rituals, and a terse 'Sod off!' was not an option.

As we got up and left the dining hall, I suddenly realised my position. I was now one of the tough kids— a cock-in-waiting. You simply did not mess with me. And as we strutted along the corridor outside, I thought that I'd better start working on a sneer. A sneer that would let passers-by know that we could strut anywhere we damn well chose, but we just happened to have chosen this squalid little corridor to strut down, *and what the hell did you intend to do about it?*

On arrival at t'bog we entered the end cubicle, because everyone knew that that was where the tough kids shat. Mark lowered his pants and eased himself onto the icy seat, yelping in an off-hand manner to indicate that he didn't have to yelp, but had actually chosen to.

What followed was primarily an audio experience, and although it is an author's job to show-not-tell, I will refrain from describing the event in detail and leave you to your own imagination.

At the conclusion of proceedings it dawned on me that my presence in the cubicle was not to bear witness to the functioning of Mark's plumbing, impressive though it was, but to hand him the bog roll. And because he was a folder rather than a scruncher, and expected nothing less of his cock-in-waiting, I would have asked him for an assistant, had the cubicle been big enough.

After he'd finished he allowed me to pull the chain.

To think I had started the day as someone who was permitted to sit with the nerds only by the skin of his teeth, and less than a few hours later I was practically allowed to wipe the cock's backside! My day had really picked up.

15

The Model Village

I spent the rest of the day, after Mark's invitation to join him in the cubicle, working on my sneer and pushing the chair in front of me with my feet, whether its occupant was crying or not.

When the bell tolled for the end of school, Mark swaggered over and invited me home to the Model Village with him. I gulped. But fortunately I managed to disguise my fear by pulling off a sneer of such intensity that I actually felt my ear move. Reluctantly, I agreed to go with him, figuring that my sneer was so well developed by now that I could ward off anything.

Trish came looking for me to walk home with her, but I said, between sneers, that I was going to a friend's house. She told me that I wasn't allowed and asked me what was up with my lip. But I just sneered at her and ran off before she had a chance to clout it from my face.

Few people would have dared enter the Model Village wearing a checked cap with woollen flaps for the ears, or if they did, I'm certain they didn't live to tell the tale. Fortunately I had three things going for me: I was with a future cock, I could run like the wind and I had a fully functioning sneer.

It was much colder in the Model Village than anywhere else in Maltby. The air felt heavier in there, as if somehow the coal dust beaten from carpets each spring had not fully dispersed and sat permanently above the houses to prevent the sun getting through and the damp evaporating.

At one time, the centrepiece of the Model Village was a bandstand, but it had been torn down—supposedly to bomb Germans. No one ever explained the connection to me and I'd given up trying to figure it out for myself. In its place was a grassed area, which would have been a pleasant place to sit and toot your trumpet, if it wasn't permanently smothered with low-fibre dog shit.

The Littles' house was the sort where you had to wipe your feet on the way out. It looked as if the council had condemned it, but halfway through demolition had had a change of heart and had put it up for tenancy. Near the front steps were the obligatory rusty pram and a dead bird, both of which might have been placed there to warn the stork against any other unplanned visits.

As I entered the lounge room I noticed that there was a crumpled pile of damp blankets in one of the chairs. I took it to be Mark's mother because I thought he would be unlikely to refer to a crumpled pile of damp blankets as 'Mum'.

Mrs Little was an old woman, though I suppose she can't have been beyond forty. She'd obviously had a tough life and was now looking at the world through the bottom of a bottle. Fate had dealt her a lousy hand, but to her credit she hadn't abandoned her family—just herself.

The walls of the house seemed to close in on us, and I suppose that was literally true because the previous tenants' wallpaper hadn't been stripped back, merely plastered over. In places, damp sheets hung from the walls and had obviously been slapped back into position, not with paste, but with the very moisture that had caused them to peel off in the first place.

I couldn't imagine why Mark had invited me to his house unless of course he planned on taking a bath and needed his scrotum scrubbing or something.

He took me upstairs to show me his room which wasn't a whole lot different from mine. Toys, footballs and books were strewn about the floor. The only real difference was that he had these forlorn strips of wallpaper hanging limply from the walls.

There was a coldness about the room that burned my throat and turned my breath to liquid. Given Mark's living conditions, it wasn't out of the question that I might get to be cock after all, but I was positive that, sneer aside, I didn't have it in me.

I made some excuse and ran home as fast as I could. My bottom lip quivered uncontrollably all the way.

I arrived totally breathless and found it surprisingly dark in the bramble patch.

16

Suburban Cowboy

By the time my sixth birthday came round, I had acquired my first hobby. Happily I discovered that I had a bit of talent and a lot of passion for football. My left foot was more powerful than most of the other boys' right, although, like everyone else, I was a total toe-basher. With England winning the World Cup in 1966 and Manchester United following it in 1968 with the European Cup, the nation's interest in its national game had become an obsession. Old ladies, who had once chatted mainly about meat prices and Ena Sharples' version of the common woman in *Coronation Street*, could now be heard discussing the merits of the 4-4-2 system and whether such a workman-like formation was here for the long haul. 'I'd like two black pudding, half a pound of tripe and do you think that the imposition of the contemporary defensive formation means the death knell for the orthodox winger, or do you think it opens up opportunities for the adventurous wing-back?'

Perhaps at last seeing faint reflections of himself in me, Dad brought me home a new plastic football every week. My powerful but waywardly inaccurate left foot had usually sent the previous week's ball over the fence or buried it in Trish's bramble patch.

For my sixth birthday, then, I wanted one thing only: a junior replica football kit. So one Saturday morning, Mum, Margaret Loader and I piled onto a bus and headed to Rotherham in search of one in my size. Although *I* didn't think I was a supporter, superior forces had other ideas. 'You *do* want a Rotherham United kit. All your friends will be jealous!' Mum was determined to support the local team, even it if was permanently entrenched in the lower half of the third division.

Such was Mum's influence over me that by the time we got off the bus, I was an avid Rotherham United supporter and had to be physically restrained from walking down the street chanting, 'Here we go, here we go, here we go. Here we go, here we go, here we go-oh.'

We traipsed around town for most of the morning, but the Rotherham United replica kit eluded us. Either the shopkeepers said bluntly that they didn't have one, or stared at us as if the idea of anyone volunteering to pay for one was totally insane. Mum, stubborn to the last, was adamant that Rotherham United kits existed. Her younger brother Tim had been given one when he was my age, but not ten minutes after having put it on, he'd sliced his knee open on Big Tom's allotment and needed over twenty stitches. I'd heard other stories of boys being injured while wearing a Rotherham United kit. Perhaps the same curse had fallen over the team's performance each week. Perhaps the Rotherham United kit was the fashion equivalent of desecrating Tutankhamen's tomb.

After visiting just about every shop in town including, oddly enough, several tobacconists, Mum's enthusiastic support for Rotherham United had waned a bit.

'Do you think John might like a cowboy outfit instead, Pat?' asked Margaret. She had seen one hanging in a toy shop window and was more a Doncaster Rovers fan herself anyway.

Mum's eyes lit up. 'He *would* like a cowboy outfit, Margaret. He would *love* a cowboy outfit!'

I was hauled into the toy shop by my hand, my body flying after it as if it was pumped full of helium and Isaac Newton was nothing more than a total southern tosser.

A man with a dust apron and a pipe took the outfit out of the window while Mum explained to me just how excited I was to be getting a cowboy outfit and how all my friends would be jealous and all the girls would want to be my girlfriend.

I was fitted with the works: genuine imitation suede waistcoat, holster, gun, spurs, black hat (I was a mean *hombre*), and those half trouser things tied on with tapes that cowboys wore so they could flash their bottoms at the cowfolk behind them on the dusty trail. Unfortunately I didn't realise, until I'd ventured out to plug a couple of startled neighbourly folk with my trusty six-shooter, that you were meant to wear pants under them.

Mum also bought me a pair of boxing gloves. She must have guessed that in a street-smart town like Maltby I would need to look after myself—especially if I went out dressed like that. She hadn't realised that I was evolving into a pacifist, and even if she had, she would probably have told me that it was easier to be a pacifist if you had a bit of force to back you up.

By the time we arrived home from Rotherham my ambition had changed from having the greatest left foot the football world had ever seen, to becoming a professional gunslinger.

I was six. I was fickle. It was all Mum's fault.

17

Conversations with Earwigs

I can't remember any single moment when I seemed destined to pursue a career as a writer, but Mum insists that she does. It's one of those little anecdotes mothers tell each other over afternoon tea. The incident might as well be fiction to me, but she swears it's true.

'Not "talking", she says, but "*conversations*"!'

'Never. How old was he?'

'Three he was. I went out to call him in for his dinner. More sticky date pudding?'

'Ah no, Pat, I'm watching my figure.'

'Margaret?'

'Ah go on, then. You only live once.'

'Are you sure now, Doris?'

'Ah, Pat; you're the devil herself. Perhaps just a small piece, then.'

'You make a lovely brew, Pat. Doesn't she, Violet?'

'Oh I know.'

'Well, as I was saying. I went out to call him in for his dinner.'

'Oh that's plenty, Pat, I'll ruin *my* dinner.'

'He was messing about by the fence. "I can't come in just now, Mammy," he says. I was just about to tell him to get his arse in here and get it in here now, when he says, "I'm having conversations with earwigs".'

'Never!'

'As true as I'm sitting here. Isn't it, Brendan?'

'Yuuusss,' Dad would say with one of those sharp intakes of breath the way the Irish do. Mind you, he would have agreed with her if she'd said that it would be a good idea to baste himself with marzipan and treacle and dance naked through the streets of Cleethorpes.

'And it's then that I knew he was going to be a writer.'

She would have used the same story had I ended up a window dresser or an axe-murderer. It gets dragged out every time Mum is discussing my literary endeavours. Yet, oddly enough, she never mentions the fact that between the ages of four and eleven I wandered around in a daze wondering what a "yabote" was—it apparently being something you row, row, rowed, merrily, merrily, merrily, merrily down a stream.

18

Cobblers

Another word I could never get my head around was
"cobbler's". I just could not differentiate between the
shoe-shop and the local shoe-mender. For some reason
I had grouped them both under the collective "cobbler's"; so cobblers they have remained.

Although Trish always found ways to embarrass me
when we went to buy new shoes, I actually enjoyed the
visit. The air was thick with what smelled like polished
cattle, and I suppose that's exactly what it was.

I loved looking in those angled knee-level mirrors
that were scattered about, although it was strange that
the cobbler had gone to the bother of showing you how
your new shoes would look if you lived on a steep hill.

After trying on my new shoes I would be forced to
stand up while Mum surveyed me from every conceiv-
able angle. She and the cobbler would get down on all
fours and sniff around my new shoes like dogs in a park,
totally obsessed with finding my big toe, which would

curl back on touch like a turtle into its shell. Once Mum was happy with the fit, the real punishment could begin in earnest. I would be forced to walk the length and breadth of the shop, following the tracks in the faded carpet of those who had gone before. Then I'd have to do it all over again—*without* bloody slouching this time! I didn't have the debating skills to convince Mum that my feet were the same size whether I slouched or not. And I didn't want to be clouted either. My embarrassment at having to go for a second *tour de shop* was made worse by the fact that there always seemed to be a good-looking girl from my class, in buying ballet shoes. And Trish, who was usually lurking near the boot section, would lunge at me with a shoehorn as I passed, or make cutting remarks about how I had to walk around the shop again and *stop bloody slouching*.

Whatever Mum got out of watching me trek across the carpet I don't know. It certainly wasn't to determine whether the shoes actually fitted, because times being what they were, practicality was always more important than comfort. I would flap around the cobbler's in my oversized shoes that I would eventually 'grow into', looking like a scuba diver and trying to avoid the boot section, because Trish and the good-looking girl from my class had teamed up to snigger at me for being such a complete plonker. Then I would have to make a third and fourth trip—'Because *I* bloody said so!'—and duck shoehorns and freshly extracted bootlaces as they were flung and flicked at me from all quarters.

Luckily, my head was encased in its checked shell and all I could feel was the distant flick of lace or horn on cap—although the design and texture of it, especially the woollen flaps for the ears, brought fresh howls of laughter from the boot section every time I passed.

19

Down Under

Visit any house in England and the talk will eventually turn to Australia, albeit to the stereotypes of kangaroos, koalas, corked hats, 'G'day, mate's, and that side-splitter about the dangers of having all that blood rush to our heads when we walk our wallabies to Bondi Beach upside-down.

My brother Paul sprang from the bramble patch one night late in the sixties, and I wondered how Trish felt about this and whether the poor little guy would be in any danger as a result. Not long after he joined us and my hearing had been restored, talk of Australia became more common in our house. It wasn't about marsupials, ridiculous headwear and walking upside-down, though. Most of the talk was about hostels, houses, employment and education. Change was in the air and from where I was standing it didn't smell too good.

I asked Mum where Australia was. She told me that it was a long way away. This didn't help. Skegness was a long way away as far as I was concerned. Ireland was on another planet—you had to go over the clouds to get there.

I asked her to be more specific. In other words, I looked vacant and dribbled. She told me that Australia was on the other side of the world and, if the government accepted us, we would get there on a 'great big massive' ship. I didn't know who this government bloke thought he was, to decide our fates just like that, but this was the least of my worries. I walked off totally confused while my mind tried to come to terms with this new information. The other side of the world? The world I lived on was flat and ended at Skegness in the east and Morecambe in the west. Ireland was somewhere up in the sky.

I stared at the ground. The other side of the world must have meant the other side of the grass, which, if you had to go there, would be through a series of tunnels. But on a ship? How was that meant to work? Was it going to flip over once we were out of sight of Skegness and sail upside-down? Or did it go down a special waterfall and then turn around and come back? I suppose Mum and Dad were too busy working out how they were going to house, feed, clothe and educate us once we got to Sydney to realise that I was having a lot of trouble with the whole idea of Australia. I decided to settle on a waterfall before turning my attention to more pressing matters—namely how were we going to live in a place that was so upside-down it was called Down Under.

I supposed we would be okay in our house because it would obviously be attached to the earth. Once inside we could walk down the up stairs and sleep peacefully on the ceiling, provided of course that the house didn't have a creaking eighth step of its own. The idea of outside, though, had me completely baffled. How would you walk around or ride a bike or play football without falling off the world? I finally settled on the idea that everyone was given specially spiked shoes that dug into the ground. There wasn't any concrete in Australia, everyone knew that, so with those spikes on you could walk everywhere; or go on walkabout, as they seemed to call it.

Paul was going to have trouble because spiked shoes were far too dangerous to give to babies. So I hoped Mum and Dad would hang onto him, tie him to a tree, or keep him in a box or something; because although I adored the little guy, I was relying on him to draw some of Trish's fire and I prayed that Australia had some good quality boxes or trees where he would be safe until he was old enough to be fitted with his own spiked shoes.

Later I asked Mum if we would be able to see kangaroos in Australia. She told me that there were millions of them in the Outback. I thought Australia was a simply brilliant place where you just had to go and look "out'back" to see all the kangaroos you wanted. All that was "out'back" of our house, apart from the little hill and Trish's bramble patch, was some mad old geezer in the house behind, who constantly flouted all firearm laws and the concerns of the British Ornithological Society's local branch by blasting from the sky anything with a pulse and a plumage.

I wondered what sort of spikes kangaroos were fitted with or whether they relied on some sort of natural suction pads on the bottom of their feet. But this was all getting too much for my mind to deal with and I went to bed promising Michael that I wouldn't let him fall off the earth in Australia, and if he wasn't given any spiked shoes of his own I would tie him to a tree or keep him in a box.

My parents have always maintained that the drug culture of the sixties totally passed them by, but I'm not convinced. Their only daughter did her Norman Bates impersonation whenever an opportunity presented itself, while I clearly had a mind that sat somewhere between Jim Morrison's and Swiss cheese.

20

T'rah, then

Even though it was a council house, Mum and Dad kept our home in immaculate condition—apart from the obligatory one drawer in the sideboard into which went everything from playing cards to batteries, unflattering photos and pen lids. Mum liked everything in its place.

Unlike me, Dad had been blessed by the handyman fairy at birth. My method these days for fixing a leak in the roof is to climb up into the loft, locate the drip, place a bucket underneath it and climb down, telling my wife Jacqui that I'm not totally useless after all. Then I wander around for the next few months, wondering where all the buckets have got to. Dad, on the other hand, would replace the roof while he was up there and take time out to add on another floor while he was at it.

At our house in Maltby, Dad had filled in and patched spaces where once there'd been doors, and cut doors where once there'd been walls. It was not uncommon for Trish and me to race through the house and smash into a wall, absolutely certain that there had been a door there that morning. The Irish and the Brits are forever having things "knocked through". You can visit a house at random and five minutes after you've been served tea and digestive biscuits, the oldest male in the house will tell you about his plans to knock through a series of walls so the vista of the back lawn can be enjoyed from any room in the house—including the cellar. Then he will tap his pipe and start complaining about the weather.

I always hoped that my dad's skills would somehow be passed on to me so that one day I too could look at a hole in a wall and proudly say, 'I knocked that through', before tapping my pipe and looking out thoughtfully at the sky. Sadly, though, it was not to be. It took me eleven hours to assemble an easy-to-erect dog kennel, and I'd practically gone insane by the time my brother-in-law came to my aid and finished the job. But on top of that, our dogs flatly refused to move in until it had passed a safety inspection check. Dad's sureness of hand seems to have skipped me and gone straight to Paul. He can actually design and put up a retaining wall and operate a fourteen-day timer on a VCR, while I lapse into a tirade about how you're better off consulting a clairvoyant than a tv guide, since they only extend to six days, tops.

But I'm digressing.

All that remained in our home in Maltby when it was time to go were a couple of carpets and echoes.

The carpets had been thoughtfully rolled up by Mum and Dad so that the new tenants could place them wherever they saw fit, and Trish and I left echoes of ourselves as we tore through the empty house, watchful in case a wall suddenly lunged out at us—the walls vibrating to our shrills, our footfalls clattering up the chimney.

By this time I had moved away from Mark Little and the cocks-in-waiting and had drifted back to my old friends. None of them believed that I was actually going to Australia so I never really got to say goodbye and that is a bit sad, I suppose. If they have any memory of me at all—and I doubt it—it would be of a skinny little kid who wore one of those checked caps with the woollen flaps for the ears, who one day simply didn't turn up for school anymore, because he was dead or something. To be fair, I don't remember much of them either. One was called Shaun, another Peter and one of them looked like a shark. Our friendships, like those of most six-year-olds, depended not on shared political, sporting or artistic beliefs, but rather on our having similar sorts of pencil cases.

What happened to any of the cats that we owned at the time I don't know. I vaguely remember Mum talking about them going to Grandad's allotment. I didn't know anything about euphemism, so I assumed that this was going to be a pleasant experience for them, and could picture mice in smoking jackets and pigs in waistcoats and top hats, greeting them as they arrived.

We spent our last night in England at Grandma and Grandad Kennedy's house on Nelson Road, too excited to sleep much beyond nine or ten hours.

The following morning it was dark, it was bleak, it was cold, it was raining. It was the perfect day to be emigrating to Sydney.

Harry Loader, bless him, had acquired a van so he could ferry us to Doncaster railway station, and the five of us piled in, along with as many Kennedys and Loaders as he could fit without calling the *Guinness Book of Records*. Considering what was to follow I remember very little about this early part of the journey, except that the side of my face was totally numb, and that's hardly surprising since it was wedged tight against the frozen window.

Doncaster station was dark and desolate when we arrived. A howling wind whipped between the platforms and freezing rain made tiny indentations on whatever skin was carelessly exposed.

Given the distance and significance of the journey that lay ahead, it would have been poignant to spot the steam from our train as it belched its way towards us through the low lying hills around Doncaster. Instead the train pulled into the station with a sort of electrified fart, which totally ruined the moment for us and undermined any romance that one of us might try to write into the scene at some later date.

With a sort of sniffling 'T'rah, then,' Trish and

Catherine said their goodbyes while the adults said theirs. I suppose I was given kisses, hugs and pats on the head, but I can't remember any. I was far too excited at getting the feeling back in my cheek, and at the prospect of the long journey ahead.

My most enduring memory of leaving England is of Catherine Loader standing on Doncaster railway station, in her fluorescent orange bear-mending wool cardigan, crying her eyes out. And, given the brightness of that cardigan, I imagine the same memory is burned deep into anyone else who was on the train with us that day.

That memory aside, I thought Trish and Catherine were just being incredibly girly. Maybe since they were older, they were more aware of the huge distance between Maltby and Sydney than I was. For me a huge distance was a trip to Skegness on a rainy day in the back of the Loaders' Austin 1100, with Trish trying to claw tattoos into my arms. Though, even after I've sailed halfway around the world and flown right around it a number of times since, the troubled road to Skegness is still my yardstick.

As the train commenced its long *clickety-clack* towards London, Trish and I slept, read, played I-spy and coloured in until a couple of hours had passed and we could no longer see the glow of Catherine's cardigan in the morning sky. We were a long way between homes.

We were travelling to Australia on an assisted passage, which meant we were the original ten-pound tourists. What I still don't know is whether the Australian Government paid to get us, or the British Government paid to get rid of us.

We arrived at Kings Cross station late in the morning. I was desperate to go to the toilet by this time and I was seriously worried just how much more my bladder would be able to take before bursting all over Trish which, karma notwithstanding, would simply have been the end of me.

I could have gone to the toilet on the train, I suppose, but my aim had always been spectacularly bad. I wasn't wide enough to anchor myself to the walls with my elbows, which was the standard practice for British Rail commuters (and you thought you were the only one) so I crossed my legs and hung on.

Reading the signals, Mum ordered Dad to take me into the toilets while she arranged tea and buns. She is English; it's in her blood.

I was standing by the trough, sighing with relief, whistling and looking at the interesting mould patterns on the ceiling, when the blood-curling roar of a lion suddenly burst out of one of the adjoining cubicles. I looked up at Dad in sheer terror while he looked down at me with the same expression on his face. I didn't know what would lead a man to make such a primordial roar, though it probably had something to do with fibre.

The last daylight that we were to experience over

England for a very long time trickled out of the sky somewhere between London and Southampton later that afternoon. Unfortunately, I missed the intense symbolism of this event because I'd fallen asleep.

It wasn't until our train pulled into Southampton and I saw how enormous our ship was that the significance of the journey we were about to take finally dawned on me. My Uncle Albert had made a pinprick on the globe just to the right of Sheffield to show me where Maltby was. Then he indicated its relationship to Skegness and Sydney. Gravity and spiked shoes were no longer a concern. Somehow it all seemed to make sense and the bottom line was that my country was being taken from me.

Never again would we walk to Stainton pub on lazy Sunday afternoons and sit in the beer garden enjoying a bag of crisps and a bottle of something fizzy while Mum and Dad went inside and got completely rat-arsed. Never again would I ride on top of a double-decker bus totally bemused as Mum did the sign of the cross with each approaching corner. Never again would I journey to Rotherham expecting to come back looking like George Best, but returning as John Wayne. Never again would I put together a birthday party list, worrying whether the invitee had ever been or was ever likely to be a classroom shitter. There were so many nevers that I felt totally choked.

I picked up Michael, being extra careful in case his

head should suddenly fall off and Mum had forgotten to bring her orange bear-mending wool, and trudged off towards the ship. The magnificent downcast character I'd created only slightly undermined by the fact that I was wearing one of those checked caps with woollen flaps for the ears.

The *Achille Lauro*

21

Cast Off

Trish and I had our noses pressed hard up against the window of the embarkation lounge, but no matter how we contorted our faces we still couldn't see the whole ship. While Dad nursed Paul, Mum came over and joined us by the window and with a typical Yorkshire penchant for exaggeration and tautology announced that the *Achille Lauro* was a great, big, bloody, massive thing. On this occasion I was inclined to agree with her: it was great, it was big, it was massive, and, when a few weeks later a demented Italian doctor finished attacking my infected toe with a scalpel, it was bloody too.

It must have been close to midnight when we were finally guided down into the bowels of the ship. We went down so many flights of stairs that it seemed as though we were on the harbour floor.

By way of conversation, Giovanni, our steward, told me that we had the same name. *Yeah right. John—Giovanni: real close, buddy.* I'd decided that my wet personality would be no use to me in Australia so I was experimenting with a new one more suited to the rugged climate of my intended country.

Giovanni showed us the wardrobe to hang our clothes in and *stow* our suitcases before he said good-night. (I was really getting into this shipspeak and couldn't wait to tell a scurvy dog to swab them decks.) We stood there in the wardrobe wondering whether Giovanni had gone off to get some coathangers when it dawned on us that the wardrobe was in fact our cabin; something that should have been apparent from the outset, given that not even Italian shipbuilders would install portholes in cupboards.

"Small" was not the word for our cabin. If you had tried to swing a cat in it, the poor thing would have been dead with massive internal injuries before you'd turned half a circle. There were two bunks, a cot for Paul, a cupboard, a porthole with a cover over it, and a bathroom that was almost indistinguishable from a box, except that people don't usually put taps in boxes.

It had been the longest day of all our lives, but Mum managed to call on her remaining reserves of energy to pack our things away and get Trish, Paul and me ready for bed. She tucked the three of us snugly in and told us that she and Dad were just popping up on deck for a bit. *Popping up?* It would have taken crampons, grappling hooks and a team of Sherpas just to get off our deck. Trish and I said we would like to go up as well to say goodbye to England, but Mum said that we would still be able to see it in the morning and that we could say our farewells then.

As the *Achille Lauro* was tugged slowly away from the dock I would like to think that Mum and Dad gave each other a hug and said something symbolic about casting off the old life and setting sail for the new. But they probably just went outside for a fag, and, after the day they'd just had and considering the unknown future that lay ahead, I can hardly blame them.

I woke about an hour or two later; I was being tossed around my bunk, not violently but with a steady rhythmic sway that would have been comforting if it wasn't so terrifying. I wasn't used to my bed heaving like that, even with Trish up to no good. It was then I remembered that I wasn't at home in Maltby anymore but on a great, big, bloody, massive ship heading for a gigantic waterfall. No one had told me that it would do this. I was terrified that the ship would turn over and hurl all of us flailing into the bitterly cold English Channel. So each time we swayed to one side a bit more than usual, I leant to the other side and raised my leg to restore the balance. I knew that my leg wasn't much of a counterweight for 50 000 tonnes of pitching steel, but no doubt every bit helped. In the weak light that was sliding under our cabin door, I noticed that Dad, more attuned to ocean travel than me, was raising his leg too, so I drifted off to sleep.

Next morning I woke to find that Dad had done his job and that the *Achille Lauro* was still afloat. Trish and I quickly got changed and raced up on deck. The air was bracing to say the least and its smell remarkable because there wasn't any. I'd never smelt air that wasn't in some way tainted with coal. Although I'd experienced sea air before, it was usually overpowered by the aroma from flasks of tea, egg sandwiches, Blackpool Rock and scones. Even then, its passage up my nostrils was usually blocked by built-up Maltby muck. Now that the crisp, clean air had a direct route to my brain, it was almost too much to deal with. I was like a native of the Amazon dragged out of the jungle and dumped in the middle of Sao Paulo by a Discovery Channel crew. My left eyelid started flickering and I developed one of those ice-cream headaches.

The *Achille Lauro* surged through the water, first churning up and then leaving behind a torrent of white-wash. It had never occurred to me that there could be no land in sight, and yet here we were, standing at the stern, or the blunt end as the English wags called it, with nothing but sea in every direction.

Trish and I pressed ourselves against the railings and gazed at the horizon until our eyes dried, but England was no more. The dark night had devoured it. We never did get to say goodbye. I'd like to think that Trish and

I gave each other a hug and said something symbolic about casting off the old life...but of course we were English and if one of us had attempted such a public show of emotion, the other would have quickly hurled the culprit overboard. Fortunately we were saved from having to do anything symbolic because it was children's feeding time so we bolted for the dining room like a pack of ravenous wolves and didn't spare another thought for dear old Blighty.

We settled into life on board quickly. Dad resisted the temptation to move any doors or threaten to knock anything through, which came as a relief because our cabin was on the side of the ship

Despite the heaving swell, which laid Dad low for a few days, Trish and I soon found our sea legs. In the morning Mum opened the cabin door and we would flutter like pigeons out into the world and return only at nightfall. 'Ding dong, ding dong. Your nose is that long' (The adults used to say this in the mistaken belief that they were being funny.) The gong would summon us from the Underworld below decks up to the enormous dining room for feeding. If we happened to run into Mum and Dad about the ship we would give a 'Hey up' and be met with a friendly, 'What devilment are you pair up to, then?' and we would tell them in great detail how we'd sat on the deckchairs and thought our thoughts and played deck games like shuffleboard, shuttlecock and our particular favourite called let's-see-who-can-hurl-the-most-quoits-overboard.

The further south we sailed, the warmer the sun felt on my face. My skin tone turned slowly from fluorescent blue to a slight pallor. I'd never felt so healthy.

On about the sixth day, when I could actually feel my ears, I realised that it was time to finally let the old life go. Because of all the excitement of exploring the ship I'd only felt vague twinges of homesickness for Maltby. But while Trish was below exploring the mayhem that could be wreaked upon the previously undiscovered and blissful playroom, I stood at the stern and contemplated my loss. I'd lost, or at least I was destined to lose, one of the most ridiculous accents in the world. I already missed Margaret Loader's kindness and Harry's hilariously bad driving (even a six-year-old could see that the best way to avoid the oncoming traffic was to scoot over to the left-hand side of the road, rather than close your eyes and hope for the best). I missed Catherine Loader and those parting tears (still) burned on my memory. I missed discussing the serial misfortunes of Rotherham United with Keith Loader. I missed Grandma's scones and her 'What's the matter then?'s. I missed walking down the street with Big Tom, knowing that nothing could hurt you when you were protected by a giant. I missed my Uncle Tim and his hilarious stories of life down t'pit and his fishing for blind mullet. I missed Jacqueline and Aunt Mary and

Uncle Tom, who at six foot five himself was the only person who could make Big Tom (his father) look like a robust hill. I missed my aunts Imelda, Dympna, Sheila and Cathleen, and uncles Eddie and Albert, whose smile could light up the gloomiest night. I was never going to be an apprentice footballer with Leeds United, Rotherham United, Doncaster Rovers, Sheffield United or Sheffield Wednesday or wear the three lions on my chest, because this was it. There would be no getting to Sydney, not liking it and then taking the next ship home. This was for keeps.

I looked out over the railings again as the horizon devoured the wash churned up by the *Achille Lauro's* propellers. Somewhere over that misty line bobbed the land that to this day I still refer to as home. And in the near distance, because this *was* forever, bobbed my checked cap with woollen flaps for the ears.

22

She's Back

And on the seventh day she discovered the playroom, and there was much wailing and gnashing of teeth.

Because we'd been yanked so forcibly from our home, not even Trish was her sure-footed and fisted self at first. Instead she turned to me for companionship, which I readily gave for fear of being bundled into a sack and sent to sleep with the grey nurse sharks. I felt as if I was living in an Indian summer, though, and pretty soon Trish's true self would rise up and lour over us before unleashing its fury.

While I was up on deck first looking for her and then having my junior existentialist crisis, Trish had stumbled across the playroom. She took an instant dislike to this French boy. He had got her hackles up not only because he couldn't speak English and had bad breath, but because he was dressed in an ill-advised little sailor suit. Although she wasn't familiar with baseball terminology, I'm certain Trish felt that he'd had his three strikes. The poor kid might just as well have walked into the play-room with a sign around his neck that said, "Please feel free to pound the hell out of me. I deserve it". Ten minutes after Trish entered the playroom, the poor kid dashed from it, sobbing in French—minus his sail-shaped hat and several oversized buttons.

Trish, it must be said, was not the least bit racist. She believed in hammering everyone equally. She was just as likely to pull the pigtails of a little Indian girl as she was to drop the shoulder into two Italian brothers who had wandered into the playroom in bow ties and quite laughably expected to leave with them on. It didn't matter if you were from Cleethorpes or Capri, Doncaster or Denmark, Bolton or Bombay, Tickhill or Turkey; if you ventured into the playroom, you were fair game.

Trish could clear a room like a dog scattering seagulls on a beach and remains to this day the only child to have ever been banned from the *Achille Lauro* playroom.

Until we discovered it, that playroom had been a perfect microcosm. Children from every economic, racial, religious, social and political background played together in complete harmony—and then a British girl in a fluorescent orange cardigan with a strange phobia of buttons came along and annexed the lot.

23

Out of the Closet

Just down the corridor from us was an Anglo-Italian couple called Justine and Stefano, who became friendly with Mum and Dad because they sat with them at dinner. They had two children our age called Gabrielle and Christopher, who Mum decided were our friends— 'Because *I* said so'. Despite the fact that they looked a bit twee to us, or at least they did to Trish (they looked rather nice to me—more on that shortly) we did become pals. Our twosome became a foursome and then a five-some, when Caroline Walton joined us.

We all avoided the playroom in protest when Trish was banned—that French kid, for example, simply had no right to turn up again in a three-piece suit and prac-tically demanded to be pushed headfirst down the slide into a strategically placed set of building blocks. So, like cats in a pantry, we prowled all over the ship—with the exception of the playroom. We relaxed in deckchairs, the "foreign" sun turning our complexions from white to pink to red and then back to white again as we were liberally doused with calamine lotion to ease the pain of our burns. We hurled quoits overboard and splashed about in the kiddie pool, once Trish had cleared it for our private use. We dropped things over the bow (sharp end) and then raced to the stern (blunt end) to see if we could spot them in the surging foam. This practice did not go down at all well with the deck crew or the poor kid whose shoe or bow tie happened to be bobbing towards the horizon.

My favourite game of all was hide-and-seek, which, given the size of the *Achille Lauro,* could literally go on all day unless the seekers got fed up, in which case the seekers became the sought. The rules were simple: girls versus boys. The seekers counted to a hundred in Gabrielle and Christopher's cabin while the sought tore off to hide. One day Christopher had a stroke of genius: we hid around the corner from their cabin and when Trish, Gabrielle and Caroline emerged and raced off down the corridor to look for us, we slipped back inside the cabin and hid in the bathroom. Christopher was so excited at having outfoxed them that he promptly tore off all his clothes as if to demonstrate how confident he was that we wouldn't be found. I shared his confidence and promptly shed my clothes too in a show of solidarity. But suddenly the bathroom didn't seem daring enough, so he gestured for me to follow him. Leaving our clothes on the bathroom floor, we walked back out into the cabin and squeezed into the cupboard. We leapt in and out a couple of times as if to drive home the point. We were in there in the pitch dark, giggling like crazy when our eyes widened to the size of startled hubcaps as the door to the cabin creaked open.

'*I didn't know these stories were true, until the other day. My friend Christopher and I were hiding naked in the wardrobe, as we often do on Thursdays, when our sisters came into the room. The thought of being discovered by them in such a compromising position only served to raise the level of excitement that was already surging behind the formica doors*'. That's from the Kentucky edition of *Penthouse*, by the way.

'They probably think they're really clever and have doubled back to hide in here.'

'They wouldn't have, Trish,' said Gabrielle. The pounding of our hearts almost deafened us. 'Christopher knows were not supposed to be in here without Mum and Dad.'

I could have kissed Gabrielle. Actually I would have *loved* to kiss Gabrielle and would have preferred to have been undressing in the bathroom and hiding naked in the wardrobe with her; but when you're six you take whatever's on offer—which isn't much. And as it was fifteen years or so before I had another experience that involved jumping naked in and out of wardrobes, I was happy to carve a notch on my bedpost, even if it was brass.

24

The Great, Big, Massive Grey Nurse

Our only European stop on the voyage was Italy, as the *Achille Lauro* made for her home port, perhaps to stock up on quoits, most of which had been Hansel-and-Gretelled overboard between Southampton and Gibraltar.

We steamed into the Mediterranean with Gibraltar on our port side and everyone leaning over the rails completely hypnotised by what was just a rock. It wasn't possible to sail on through the Mediterranean and take the Suez Canal shortcut because it was still closed to traffic after the Six Day War. So we would have to go back out again into the Atlantic and sail round the Cape of Good Hope. Having no concept of geography, though—I was still waiting for that huge waterfall to loom up in front of us—I was surprised when a week or so later we sailed past an entirely different Gibraltar on our starboard side that equally fascinated all those on board. I couldn't work out why these Gibraltars so intrigued everyone, because at the current rate we were bound to run across at least half a dozen more before we arrived in Sydney.

As we entered the calmer waters of the Mediterranean, the cover that had been kept on for the rougher North Atlantic, was removed from our porthole and I finally got to see what the world looked like through a round window. Well, it was brilliant. Water, buoys, seabirds, ships, islands and foreign lands drifted past my bedroom as if on God's conveyor belt. And unless the people over the road from us in Maltby had access to some seriously high-grade LSD, then my view was certainly superior to anything drifting past theirs.

We docked in Genoa and then Naples and although my six-year-old's memory has fused them into one stopover, I remember liking Italy very much. The Italians obviously enjoyed life, while for the English it was there to be endured. Here were people who took a three-hour lunch break so that they could eat, drink, listen to music, play football or *bocce*, read, sleep and shag and speak with their arms.

Many of the English on board openly loathed the Italians, or "Eyeties" as they called them with a slight sneer. Some would never forgive fascist Italy her role in "The War", while others found it unforgivable that Italy had changed sides only when victory for the Allies was assured. Some went as far as to openly admit that they preferred Germans. 'You knew where you stood with the Krauts. Okay, the Nazis might have been deranged, genocidal psychopaths, but at least they got the trains to run on time.'

Disembarking in Naples, Dad decided that we needed to find a Catholic church. Obviously our souls were awash with nautical sins. Fortunately I wasn't a confirmed Catholic and that meant I didn't have to go to confession. This came as a bit of a relief because even though Giovanni was teaching me and Trish Italian, I was fairly sure that my new language skills didn't stretch to asking to be absolved for jumping naked in and out of wardrobes.

Dad asked a street-stall vendor where the nearest church was. I'm not sure how well the Southern Irish brogue translates into Neapolitan, but as the man set about giving Dad animated directions he looked like he was trying to break a toffee with his butt cheeks. The nearest Catholic church was clearly two light years from the Horsehead Nebula and to get there we had to leap off Vesuvius and flap like Icarus.

Dad thanked the vendor for his time and performance and then felt obliged to buy something from him. Although a statuette of Our Lady wasn't exactly in Our Budget, it did have the bonus of a battery-operated light.

With the Blessed Virgin safely wrapped in brown

paper and tucked in Mum's handbag, which hardly seemed fitting travel arrangements for the mother of the Church, regardless of the thirty-watt bulb up her clacker, we set off for the Horsehead Nebula and ended up paying homage at a church that we stumbled across along the way.

Eventually we met up with some of Mum and Dad's friends from the ship one of whom, Harold Bamford, spoke fluent Italian. He had been incarcerated in Italy during the war. Uncle Gagald, as Paul called him, gave us a wonderful tour of the city. I learned something about human nature—the nature I knew I'd like to have, anyway—from watching this little old English guy speaking in such fluent and friendly terms with the locals, while everyone else in our group looked on with deep mistrust. Even at six I could see that Uncle Gagald wasn't talking to bloody, filthy, back-stabbing Eyeties, who you could trust about as far as you could spit, but to lively, passionate, friendly people who could teach the English a thing or two about living.

Back on board, we were all up on deck when a "huge, big, massive, dirty, great shark" surfaced beside the ship. Suddenly everyone went from being total berks to expert icthyologists. After a heated debate, the shark was declared a grey nurse because it was grey and had a little watch on its chest I guess. I'm certain that most of their previous exposure to sharks would have been as a side order with chip butties: the popular Friday night treat.

Now we were getting conversations along the lines of, 'You can tell from the markings on its dorsal fin that it has recently been involved in a territorial dispute with a great white, or, to give its Latin name, quote *Carcharodon carcharias* unquote, and has followed the coastal stream of North Africa in search of new breeding slash feeding grounds'.

I think it was a blind mullet myself.

There was talk of getting a gun or something sharp to hurl at the thing so that we could all admire it at closer quarters. Some of the older boys started throwing quoits at it because although sharks are at the business end of the food chain and have no real enemies in the ocean, everyone knows that they live in morbid fear of deck game accessories, and it smartly disappeared under the murky waters of Naples Harbour.

25

I'm with Stupid

The most magical stop on the voyage was the island of Tenerife. We arrived late at night but Tenerife simply woke up to greet us. Street-stalls lit up like the fairy lights at Christmas time in Sheffield at the influx of sterling, as the Brits, second only to Americans, went about maintaining their reputation as connoisseurs of all things kitsch. They bought armfuls of t-shirts printed with witty slogans like "I've been to Tenerife, so bollocks to you!" or "I'm with Stupid". There weren't many fish-and-chip stalls in Tenerife, so we had to watch a number of our countrymen hacking their way back to the ship through thickets of cliché as only the British abroad can. 'I'm not touching any of that foreign muck. Give me half a pound of cold tripe and lashings of sheep's brains and I'm sorted.'

We walked up through the tight streets and looked down at the harbour and our magnificent home nestling snugly against the dock. As we began the long walk back, though, I noticed that the *Achille Lauro*'s twin funnels were billowing smoke and naturally assumed it was leaving without us.

I didn't know anything about departure times and thought we were going to be stuck forever in Tenerife and be forced to eat loads of foreign muck and wear "I'm with Stupid" t-shirts. When I voiced my concerns, Mum looked at me and said, 'No, darling. The ship's not going without us. The captain's just turned on the funnels to warm up our beds.' That remains to this day one of the loveliest things I have heard.

26

Kids Overboard

Not long after we left Tenerife there was an announcement over the PA system telling us all to go back to our cabins and prepare for the lifeboat drill. Having clambered in and out of a few lifeboats during our games of hide-and-seek, I thought I would be well placed to give Mum and Dad some advice about what they would have to do.

Trish and I returned to the cabin to find the porthole cover closed—the heavy seas were giving the ship a battering—and Mum and Dad with matching long faces. I wondered briefly if they had discovered Christopher naked in our wardrobe, but we'd ceased that practice some time before because it was a bit suss.

'What's the matter?' Trish asked.

'Put your life vests on and sit down,' said Mum. 'We have to tell you something.'

They helped us into our life vests and we sat meekly

on Trish's bottom bunk knowing full well that something was up.

'You know that it's the lifeboat drill today?'

We nodded.

'Do you know what you have to do, though?'

We shook our heads. Dad stood to one side with a priestly demeanour. He was wearing a brown skivvy and looked a lot like Daniel Day Lewis would years later during the filming of *The Unbearable Lightness of Being*. In fact if it hadn't been for the bright orange life vest, the resemblance would have been uncanny.

Mum timed a pause as deftly as Dietrich, and Trish and I started to panic.

'Well,' she finally continued, 'they haven't lost anyone yet.'

Our faces fell like anvils from a bridge. *Lost anyone?*

'Whherrellld...?'

'What do you mean they've never lost anyone?' said Trish. I'd lost the power of speech. 'What do they do to you?'

'Well, they have to make sure that your life vest works.'

'Whherrellld...?'

'How do they do *that*?' said Trish.

'They take you up to the front of the ship and throw you into the sea.'

'**WHHERRELLLD!**' It's hard to ask questions and

make exclamations when your bottom lip is quivering out of control.

'If anyone tries to throw me overboard,' said Trish, 'I'll claw their eyes out.'

That wasn't fair. Trish could hook her talons into anyone who tried to hurl her into the ocean, while all I could do would be to hit them with my sneer as I sailed through the air.

'They'll put gloves on you, then,' said Mum.

'What about the propellers?' asked Trish. 'Won't we go under the ship and get chopped up?'

'No, that's okay. They use the two strongest crew men to throw you as far out as possible.'

'How do you get back on t'ship?' I asked, hugging Michael.

'There's a man at the back with a great, big, massive pole who hooks you back on board.'

'What about Paul?'

'They have a special scoop for babies.'

'What if he misses?'

'Oh there'll probably be another ship along eventually.'

'But what about grey nurse sharks?' I blurted through my rising panic.

'If they miss you they throw you a stick so you can whack sharks on the nose. Sharks don't like being hit on the nose. I read that somewhere.'

Yeah, and kids didn't relish the thought of being hurled

overboard from about six storeys up and nothing but a guy
with a net and a stick to stop them being eaten by sharks.

So that was that. We were having none of it. We clung
to our bunks like cats to a rug on a cold winter night.

'C'mon, we've got to go.'

'No!'

'Tickle his feet, Brendan. He doesn't like that.'

'No!'

'It'll all be over before you know it.'

'No!'

'And you can have a nice cup of tea to warm you
up afterwards.'

'Shove your tea!' said Trish.

Mum burst out laughing. 'With margarine and
buttons.'

Trish stabbed her with dagger eyes.

'No!' I was still a few sentences behind.

'You're joking, aren't you?' said Trish.

'Of course we're joking.'

'C'mon, John,' said Trish. 'It's okay. They're pulling
our legs.'

'I don't have to be thrown into the sea with all the
grey nurse sharks?'

'No, you don't.'

Mum held out her hand. 'C'mon, lovey.'

'You leave him alone!' snapped Trish. She held out
her hand and led me up on deck with our well and truly
chastened parents sniggering in our wake.

27

The Lion at the Centre of the Earth

A few days after the dramatic lifeboat drill, everyone was up on deck on a glorious sunny morning. We were all waiting eagerly for the ship to pass over the equator. I was really looking forward to this significant event—my enthusiasm only slightly dampened by the fact that I didn't know what an equator was.

Though still wary of her since the lifeboat drill, I asked Mum—only to be told that the equator was a line at the centre of the earth. I should have asked her whether she was taking the piss or if she'd been at the ship's cooking sherry, but she seemed deadly serious.

I ran to the railing, eager to be the first to spot this lion, wondering whether it was a real lion, a statue of one, or one carved out of a mountain on an island. Perhaps it was a blow-up one, anchored in position like a buoy. I decided that it couldn't possibly be real because lions lived in jungles and went in for jumping over cameras and wrestling with Tarzan. Although I never doubted Tarzan's bravery, the mighty, muscular, fanged thing that leapt over the camera often bore little resemblance to the bathmat he finally beat the crap out of.

The captain blasted the ship's horn and everyone started cheering, clinking glasses and throwing hats in the air, but despite the on-board excitement, the lion remained annoyingly elusive.

I glanced around to see whether Mum had convinced the entire ship, captain included, to play another gag on me. But she was lying on a deckchair with a book and a fag, under the standard English impression that it was healthy to have blistered skin. So I committed the entire incident to memory to let my brain sort it out at a later date, when it had more information.

28

Of Pigeons and Albatrosses

I was sitting on a deckchair near the stern when a great, big, massive seagull landed on the railing. It glanced around, less in fear than a polite: 'Do you mind if I rest here for a bit?'

A man a few seats down from me with a flat-cap and a pipe said, 'Hello there, Mr Albatross. How are you gettin' on, then?'

Now I did know that people from Manchester knew a lot about birds, especially pigeons, but I hadn't realised that this knowledge extended to being on first name terms with every one they met.

It started to rain, so the guy tapped his pipe, said farewell to Mr Albatross and disappeared below, presumably to leaf through his back copies of the *Whippet and Pigeon Fanciers' Almanac*. I wasn't too bothered by the rain so I moved closer to Mr Albatross and had a bit of a chat—asking after his health, origins, dietary habits and so forth, before the rain increased to a heavy blatter that caused us both to flap away.

'Where do you think you've been?' said Mum, asking me the question that always confused me. 'You're wringing wet.'

'I've been up on t'deck talking to a really fat seagull called Mr Albatross.'

When Mum had recovered the power of speech and had stopped beating the floor with her fists, she sat me down and told me about albatrosses, the height they flew and the enormous distances they travelled just to get a shag—though she called it 'find a mate'. I thought about our games of hide-and-seek and doubted very much that I would travel over 8000 miles to find Gabrielle Tardelli, unless of course she was hiding naked in the wardrobe at the end of it.

29

Suth Effruca and the Fushwife

If I thought mine was bad, the South African accent was tantamount to assault. When we passed through customs in Capetown, even the Scots were sniggering as they were told, 'Wulcum to the Rupubluc uf Suth Effruca.'

Once we were cleared, we made our way out into the streets with the Tardellis and started exploring the city. I hadn't seen so many dark-skinned people since we went to Bradford. Coming from Maltby, I'd only had limited exposure to the rest of the world. I'd once answered the door as a four-year-old to a Sikh who was selling encyclopaedias. 'Who is it?' called Mum from the kitchen. Without taking my eyes off the man I yelled back to her, 'It's a Chinese man with a towel on his head'. If by some quirk of fate that man happens to be reading this, I'm really sorry—okay? I was four. It was Maltby.

As we headed for Table Mountain, we noticed that there was a demonstration taking place in the next street.

'What's going on?' I asked Mum.

'It's an anti-apartheid demonstration, lovey.' She might just as well have been speaking in Afrikaans for all the sense it made to me.

'What's that?'

'Apartheid means that black people aren't treated equally.'

'Why not?'

'I don't know.'

Neither did the rest of the world.

We left South Africa and let it get on with the business of being the arsehole of the world. It was both geographically and politically positioned for some heavy-duty colonic irrigation, but that took its time in coming. The fact that it did without full-on civil war surely places Nelson Mandela as one of the greatest leaders in history.

We set sail for Fremantle some 4600 miles away. It was going to be quite a while before we saw land again. We were on our own self-contained island drifting slowly east; like the Love Boat with rust.

Giovannni continued with our Italian lessons, but our Yorkshire accents kept getting in the way. So when we tried our new language out on another crew member, he would give us a terse 'scuzi?', point in the general direction of the playroom and then, adhering strictly to stereotype, go back to daydreaming about football, food, drinking and shagging. And there are worse stereotypes than that.

With Trish on her last probation we returned to the playroom just in time for the big fancy dress competition. Each child was given three rolls of coloured crepe paper with which to plan, design and make a costume—in Trish's case, as far away from the playroom as possible. The parade was scheduled for the following week in the dining hall-cum-auditorium in front of a packed audience, or at least anyone who felt like coming or was too drunk to leave.

Trish wanted this. She wanted it very much. So Mum beavered away day and night on Trish's creation like a demented seamstress until her fingers bled. I was less enthusiastic about the whole business, so on the day of the big parade Trish was ready and raring to take centre stage, whereas I went as something green. Though it would be hard to pinpoint her character, I suppose Trish was a sort of cleaning/washerwoman, complete with apron, mop, hairnet and cigarette, all of which—with the exception of the fag—were constructed from crepe paper. As impressive as Mum's sewing efforts were—and they *were* impressive because some of the crew asked for the pattern—it was Trish who was really going to steal the character and the show.

She rehearsed talking with the fag hanging out of

her mouth, her jaw jutting forward to aid the process
as she complained of her husband's diphtheria, her son's
rickets, and her own lumbago, all of which transpired
to make her life a total misery and prevent her from
actually doing any cleaning. She even chose to forsake
her Yorkshire accent in favour of an east Lancashire one,
so it was impossible to watch her without immediately
thinking *fishwife*.

Mothers from every nation had toiled long and hard
so that their offspring would shine in the big parade,
but to no avail, as their children just couldn't capture
the essence of the character the mothers had so painstak-
ingly created.

When my turn came, I followed a huge banana onto
centre stage, to a polite trickle of applause. I still wasn't
certain what I was supposed to be. But then from the
wings came an urgent whisper, 'You're a pirate, John,
you're a pirate. You're a *bloody* pirate! Now *act* like one!'
I turned around and skipped off stage, under some mis-
guided notion that pirates went in for skipping.

Finally it was Trish's turn in the limelight. She thundered onto the stage and started abusing the first nine
rows, 'Shut your gob, you drunken sod! You dun't know
now't. I've just about had it up to my neck with you
lot!' I'm not sure what Mum thought as she watched.
Trish continued in this vein for about five minutes until
somebody fashioned a crook and dragged her off.

She won so easily that I think she was awarded second

and third prize as well, while my pirate still haunts me. At that moment I was rather proud to be Trish's brother—a feeling that continues to this day.

Australia

30

Sun, Sand, Sea, Surf and Sinuses

To say Australia is big is a bit like saying Stephen Hawking is clever. It doesn't even come close. Maltby is nearer to the Sahara Desert than Perth is to Sydney.

Debate still rages over which European explorer "discovered" Australia. Captain James Cook (1770) is given the credit by many, and since the Cookmeister hailed from Yorkshire, I am generally in his corner. But even Cook's most ardent admirer would be forced to admit that he was hardly the first European explorer to set foot on Australian soil.

Dutchman Dirk Hartog put ashore on an island in Shark Bay, Western Australia in 1606, didn't like the look of the place, scribbled out a half-hearted message on a bit of tin, and then buggered off back to Holland, where he presumably spent the rest of his days getting off his face in various Amsterdam cafés.

In 1642 another Dutch mariner, Abel Tasman, discovered Tasmania (now there's a coincidence) but apparently failed to spot the slightly larger landmass just a little to the north.

The French were also known to have been exploring the Pacific in the 1700s and are believed to have actually sailed into Botany Bay; thought it dull on account of its lack of restaurants, cafés, nightclubs and brothels, and promptly set sail for Paris. And who can blame them?

The actual discovery of Australia by Europeans, then, is probably a moot point since our Aboriginal cousins have been here for over 60 000 years, and at over seven million square kilometres, how could you possibly miss the place?

Having not seen land for about two weeks—perhaps Abel Tasman was at the helm—we finally berthed at Fremantle in December 1969.

As we emerged from our cabin, the glare almost blinded us. Our pupils immediately shrivelled to the size of pinpricks.

A couple of old school friends of Mum's from Maltby, John and Meta Elkin, had moved to Perth the previous year and we had arranged to meet them. They collected us from the dock and took us on a wonderful tour of the city. Their eldest daughter Deborah was the same age as me and was in fact in my class at school back in

Maltby until, tragically, she died. Or so the rumour went. So it came as a pleasant surprise to find her sitting next to me in the car and not dead at all—as I'm sure it was for her. I was so glad that Deborah wasn't dead. Aside from the fact that she was rather lovely, she would shortly become the first girl I ever kissed, and I'm certain it wouldn't have been half as much fun if she was a corpse.

The Elkins took us for a run up to King's Park. We gazed down at the magnificent city of Perth and the Swan River twinkling alongside it and marvelled at how beautiful it was in comparison to, say, Scunthorpe. A couple of us wondered about house prices. One of us wondered if there were any grey nurse sharks about.

'Well, not walking around,' said John Elkin.

'I think he means in the river,' said Meta.

'Oh aye,' said John. He winked at Mum and Dad. 'They get up as far as t'sewage system. That's why they had to invent the s-bend on t'lavvy. So folks wouldn't get bitten on t'bum.'

'Give over, John,' said Meta. 'Stop tormenting him.'

Looking down on Perth, I had to admit that Australia wasn't exactly the way I'd imagined it. One of my friends from school (the one who looked like a shark, oddly enough) had told me that Australians drank green tea and couldn't walk down the street without being set upon by the snakes who pretty much had the run of the place. I thought he was off his head. From what I could gather by looking at Mum and Dad's glossy brochures, we would live in a hut near the beach and pick fallen fruit off the sand in the morning for our breakfast. Trish and I would then go to school in a surf-boat, wearing nothing but a funny little cap with strings and a pair of tiny underpants, which for some reason disappeared up your bottom. There was a man at the back of the surfboat (the headmaster, probably) who had an extra long stick that he obviously used for whack-ing grey nurse sharks on the nose. Dinner would be whatever our Aboriginal friends in the next hut had managed to spear that day, and of course more fruit. Any scraps that were left over after the meal we would throw out'back to the kangaroos. On the weekend we would round up all our sheep and take them for a run out to the desert and onto Ayers Rock in our enormous lorry.

Green tea and snakes on the street? Ha!

John and Meta set up a picnic blanket, pulled out a flask of tea and some egg and mayonnaise sandwiches and began reminiscing about the good old days with Mum and Dad.

'We used to have to wear barbed-wire wrapped round us bare feet to be able to get through pack-ice t'school.'

'*We* could never afford barbed-wire and were thrashed daily wit' headmaster's belt-buckle for being late. And that was just as well because by time we got t'lesson, half t'class had been sold t'local vivisectionist.'

We knew too well that these sessions could go on

for days, particularly if the subject of war rationing was broached. So, encouraged by Trish, I sauntered over and kissed Deborah on her cheek, and to my absolute amazement she came back for seconds.

'Our great grandad went down t'pit when he were two to be a donkey man.'

'Thee were right vindictive, them pit ponies.'

'Aye, thee were.'

'Life expectancy for a two-year-old donkey man in the eighteen hundreds were twelve minutes, and that were including morning tea break.'

'Course, though, we could never afford butter for t'sandwiches and had to use what dripping we could squeeze from Grandad's sinuses.'

I'd just had my first kiss with a gorgeous girl, and if I closed my eyes and listened to the accents damaging the air, it was as if I was back home in Maltby. My life was good because my needs were simple. Thee dun't know tha born nardays.

31

The Fairy Meadow

Sadly, the time came to leave the Elkins and we sailed across the Great Australian Bight and on to Melbourne. A friend of Mum and Dad's on board, a single guy called Big Paul (my baby brother was Little Paul), generously offered to take me and Trish to a fun park in Melbourne to give them a break from us and have a bit of a play at being a parent himself. Despite the fact that Trish was on her best behaviour, Big Paul arrived back on board the *Achille Lauro* after our four hours together, muttering 'vasectomy' over and over again. It was a new word to me.

From Melbourne, it was up the New South Wales coast and finally into Sydney Harbour early on New Year's Eve 1969. Giovanni woke us; we threw on some clothes and scampered up on deck like dogs up a rock face, eager to be the first to catch a glimpse of our new home.

We stepped out into the sharp morning air as Sydney Harbour Bridge rose before us bigger than we could ever have imagined. Living in Maltby had persuaded me that the English did things on a much more moderate scale. The biggest structure that I'd encountered up until then was the helter-skelter at Morecambe fun fair.

People pointed at the tallest skyscraper, Australia Square, and made whimsical remarks about the fact that it was round. The skyline, though much lower than it is now, was awesome, and I held onto Mum with an extra firm grip in case it swallowed me whole. Even London wasn't as impressive as this. Thanks largely to the efforts of the German Luftwaffe, developers there had been given plenty of space for low-rise expansion after the war. Sydney, on the other hand, was crowded around the cove with nowhere to go but up. We sailed breathlessly under the Bridge and docked at Pyrmont after six long weeks at sea.

Several hours later, having packed up all our belongings, we said *ciao* to Giovanni and hauled ourselves up on deck for the last time to begin the long wait for processing by immigration and customs. I guess children are just a PS on their parents' passports, so I don't remember us actually being processed, which is a bit of a shame really because in all the films you see about the Irish landing in New York, there's some burly immigration officer with a hat and a moustache stamping the migrant's passport before bestowing a warm, 'Welcome to America, the home of the free and the land of the brave', or something equally patronising.

We followed a throng of our fellow migrants out of the processing area and onto a waiting coach.

What should have been thrilling was largely anti-climactic. The ship had become our home and I for one would have been happy to keep on sailing round the world, right back home to England.

That was the last we were to see of the *Achille Lauro*. She ploughed the ocean for a number of years as a migrant-cum-cruise ship and then underwent a major refit and found new life as a luxury liner—our old cabin at last answered its calling as a wardrobe. In 1985, though, it was front page news when four terrorists seized control of my former home and shot dead an American national, Leon Klinghoffer, and threw him and his wheelchair overboard because of the obvious danger that he and it posed to their cause. Unless, of course, the unfortunate Mr Klinghoffer had accidentally run over one of the hijackers' feet, his only crime was his Jewish name. Surely not since the end of the Second World War has the saying, "What's in a name?" brought about a more heartless and cowardly act.

In 1993 the *Achille Lauro* appeared on the news one last time. Now well past her sell-by date, her engines ceased functioning off the coast of Somalia and several hours later she slipped slowly beneath the waves with nothing more than a hiss and a gurgle.

As we took our seats on the coach, I decided that Australia wasn't for me. It was too big, too fast, too hot. I wanted things to be smaller, slower, colder. I wanted the helter-skelter at Morecambe fun fair. I wanted Maltby.

As she nursed Paul, Mum gave me a warm smile. I smiled back at her and it could almost have been a scene from *The Waltons* or *The Brady Bunch,* except that my smile started in my brain and ended at my lips, whereas a real smile came from the heart and shone out through the eyes.

The coach threaded its way slowly out of the city and headed south. I have a vague memory of there being an enormous bowling pin on the side of the road some-where—advertising ten-pin bowling, no doubt—but with my head nodding like a politician talking to the Queen, that's about all I've retained of the coach ride to Wollongong.

Our destination was the Fairy Meadow migrant hostel, which sounded positively delightful. I pictured a light breeze whispering across a sun-licked, flower-dripping meadow, where enchanting pixies delivered armloads of blueberries and other assorted fruit to our quaint thatched cottage, before fashioning instruments out of seashells and playing gentle melodies to soothe us through another night in paradise.

I could have contemplated a fairy meadow until the end of time, but there's simply no way I would have arrived at a stretch of dry wasteland packed with corru-gated iron sheds that were baking under a relentless sun.

We melted off the coach and were eventually shown to our shed. We entered it with a collective sigh and immediately retreated back outside, gasping for air.

'Mortein, heh, heh, heh,' said Mr Nosepoke, our friendly park attendant, who clearly enjoyed delivering bad news. He was an English migrant himself who had been in the hostel for some time. Like us, he'd sought a better life in this colonial outpost, found it at the hostel and sought no further. Rather than laugh outright, Mr Nosepoke was one of those people who said, 'heh, heh, heh' when he thought something was funny or should have been, whereas 'hee!' conveyed concern.

'Mortein?' said Mum.

'For mosquitoes,' replied Mr Nosepoke. 'Heh, heh, heh.'

'Mosquitoes?'

'Big enough to carry you off, heh, heh, heh,' he said. 'I've sprayed your cabin, heh, heh, heh.'

I didn't have any idea what mosquitoes were, but it sounded as if only a toxic gas strike would keep them at bay.

'There's a net in your cabin that you can sleep under, heh, heh, heh. There's always more spray, heh, heh, heh.'

'So it's either get eaten alive,' said Mum, 'or suffocate in a net?'

'Heh, heh, heh. The beach is only two minutes walk away,' he said, somewhat unnecessarily, since we could see it. But we'd have to watch out for sharks, heh, heh,

heh, bluebottles, heh, heh, heh, jellyfish, heh, heh, heh, and blue-ringed octopus, which were apparently so deadly that just to look at one caused several of your limbs to fall off, hee!

My earlier idea of what Australia would be like came back to me: we would live in a hut, walk to the beach and pick fallen fruit off the sand. And apart from the fruit and being mangled by the local wildlife, it looked like I'd pretty much nailed this one.

Green tea and snakes on the street? Heh. Heh. Heh.

Mum tried to make the best of things in that "Right. Let's get cracking" English manner that Churchill had harnessed to such great effect. But no matter how much cracking she did, there was just no getting past the fact that we now lived in a shed. And Dad. Our poor dad, who had a job lined up at the Port Kembla steelworks, not only had to live in a shed; he had to go and work in a fire. He must have thought he was in hell. But not once did he complain. Not once. I thought of Maltby pit that Dad would never go down because (not unreasonably) he was afraid of closed-in spaces, and imagined that the steelworks was ten times worse. Dad was prepared to work in the furnace so that his sons wouldn't have to. Such a selfless act made him my hero, and that's what he's been ever since.

We returned to the shed and stayed for about an hour—a world record for the Fairy Meadow migrant hostel—before packing up our things again and heading back to Sydney. Providence had landed on our doorstep and our family's fortunes improved immeasurably. My own, however, were about to suffer a marked downturn.

32

The Screaming Trees

It was a new decade and our first full day in Australia and I woke to the sound of someone walking up and down the street, blowing a whistle. What strange land had I been dragged to where citizens were whistled awake and the houses only had downstairs? As another whistle shrilled along the street, I pulled back the covers and crawled out of bed. For a moment I wasn't sure where I was. But then I remembered how we had been rescued from our Fairy Meadow shed the day before by James and Mary, Irish friends of ours from Maltby, who had moved to Sydney the previous year and were living in the suburb of Georges Hall. After making the trek to Fairy Meadow to welcome us, they'd taken one look at our shed and announced that we would not be staying a minute longer while they had room in their house.

I *trip-trapped* over Trish's sleeping form and found Dad and Uncle James making tea in the kitchen. While Uncle James poured me a cup, I asked him who was outside making all that racket with the whistle. He laughed and told me that it was the paper boy. I tried as hard as I could not to imagine a boy made entirely of paper, but it wasn't easy.

Uncle James interpreted my vacant expression. 'He delivers *newspapers*.'

While Dad and he discussed job prospects, I finished my tea and then wandered out the back through the *click-clack* screen-door and found Mum and Aunt Mary hanging clothes on the weirdest looking clothesline I'd ever seen. It looked like the sort of contraption that the characters in my *Boys' Own* annuals might transform into a homemade helicopter before giving a bunch of Fuzzy Wuzzies or bank robbers a thorough sorting out.

As Mum pegged out the last sock, a breeze whipped through the clothes, so that when Aunt Mary turned the handle to raise the line higher and catch the sun, the washing began to whirl around and around—a sort of working-class spin dryer. It would be many years before I would be convinced that the Hills Hoist didn't spin when you turned the handle.

I was disappointed to discover that there weren't any kangaroos out'back of Uncle James and Aunt Mary's house. But the people over the fence did have a pool, so that looked promising. I made my way around to the front of the house from out'back. The air was thick with the buzz of blowflies adding to the drone of the aircraft taking off from nearby Bankstown Airport. The grass was scorched to straw and the clouds were remarkable for the simple reason that there weren't any. In the distance the road shimmered like the *Achille Lauro's* pool. Uncle James and Aunt Mary's house, though, was relatively cool because it was shaded by a couple of enormous trees. Trees that had a rather disconcerting habit of screaming. I was still coming to terms with paper boys, houses that only had downstairs, screen-doors that went *click-clack*, and clotheslines that spun when you turned the handle; so I was content to leave the screaming trees alone for the moment.

But out of the shade, and even this early in the morning, the sun had a bite to it. So we decided to go to the beach, because this was Sydney in the seventies and that's what you did. After breakfast, the seven of us piled into Uncle James's old EH Holden, leaping about like frogs on a barbecue as the vinyl seats seared our skin.

We cruised along Henry Lawson Drive with Bankstown Airport on our left and Georges River on our right. Just before Milperra Bridge, Uncle James pulled off the road to show us a "BEWARE OF SHARKS" sign that had been erected on the banks of the river. I wasn't sure how you went about being wary of sharks, other than staying in your house or moving back to Maltby, so I got out of the car and approached the river in a sort of alert karate pose.

'You're having us on,' said Mum as she gazed at the sign. 'They don't come up this far, surely?'

'They do,' insisted Aunt Mary. 'And further.'

'Can you believe this, Brendan?' said Mum.

'Yuuusss,' replied Dad, standing to one side and firing up a smoke.

'What sort *are* they?' said Mum. 'Grey nurses?'

'I don't think so,' said Uncle James, also lighting up. 'Grey nurses are harmless.'

'Really?' said Trish. 'We thought they were the worst ones.'

'Big kitty-cats,' said Uncle James. 'Your grey nurse is a fearsome looking creature with all those teeth. Big too. But as sharks go, they're actually quite timid. That's why they're popular with aquariums.'

Dad was being wary of sharks by sitting on the bonnet of the car, where fatal attacks were rare. 'So which ones come up the rivers?'

'Probably bulls,' said Uncle James. He took another drag on his smoke, possibly for effect. 'They're the third deadliest after white pointers and tigers.' For someone who dug up roads for a living, Uncle James seemed to know an awful lot about marine biology.

'Bull sharks?' I asked.

'Yuuusss,' said Uncle James.

I tried not to imagine a shark with horns.

Then Aunt Mary told us a story about a local woman who tried to commit suicide by jumping off Milperra

Bridge. The poor woman leapt off the bridge and landed in the jaws of a shark, which chomped off both her arms—probably in fright.

Mum joined Dad on the bonnet of the car. I resumed my karate pose. Trish edged closer to the water.

What strange land had I been dragged to where you threw yourself off a bridge, only to find yourself being half eaten by a fish?

The story had a happy ending, Uncle James assured us. The woman survived the attack.

'But she tried to kill herself,' said Trish, who was staring at the river as if daring a bull shark to chomp *her* arms off.

'That's right,' said Aunt Mary, 'but she lived.'

Like Trish, I couldn't decide whether the woman was lucky or unlucky. I also wondered how she managed to swim ashore minus her arms. But I decided to leave that with the screaming trees for the moment.

The sand was already starting to liquefy by the time we arrived at Wanda Beach about an hour or so later. The air was heavy with humidity and smelled as if someone had been barbecuing thongs in it. Surfers bobbed like otters on half-formed waves. Seagulls fell out of the sky with the sheer exhaustion of trying to stay in it. Out on the road, the sun bonded tyres to asphalt.

We lugged our picnic blanket, towels, flasks of tea, and egg and mayonnaise sandwiches down onto the molten lava and peeled off our shirts. Our fluorescent skin immediately began to sizzle like fat in a frying pan. I was worried that if it got any hotter my brain might start to boil. Mum's brain had already gone into meltdown. That's the only way I could explain what happened next.

Our previous exposure to the "surf" had been the seaside at Skegness and Morecambe, where you could bound into the water, stride out for a couple of miles and still get only your ankles wet.

But this *wasn't* the seaside at Skegness or Morecambe. If you strode out for a couple of miles here, you could very quickly find yourself half a mile under water. Provided a bull shark hadn't already made off with your arms.

Showing flagrant disregard for sunstroke, melanomas, rips, troughs, the pounding swell, and the fact that she couldn't swim, Mum stripped down to her bathers and went bounding into the surf in exactly the way that someone who'd grown up on the beaches of Skegness and Morecambe shouldn't. It hadn't occurred to her that you could drown within sight of your picnic blanket, flask of tea, and egg and mayonnaise sandwiches. It occurred to her now, though.

Fortunately for Mum, Uncle James was a powerful swimmer and had bounded into the surf himself a few moments earlier. As Mum went surging past, Uncle James managed to stick out an arm and pull her to safety. In her panic, though, rather than thank Uncle James for saving her life, she clawed at him until his back looked like somebody had set about him with a cat o' nine-tails. When the lifesavers arrived they didn't know whether Mum had been caught in a rip, or Uncle James had been mauled by a determined one-toothed shark.

We drove home in a subdued and reflective mood: a combination of sunburn, sunstroke, heat exhaustion, Uncle James's wounds and Mum having almost been carted off to New Zealand.

I wondered whether Mum had had enough of Australia with its troughs, rips, paper boys, houses that only had downstairs, screen-doors that went *click-clack*, clotheslines that spun when you turned the handle, screaming trees and sharks that chomped off your arms when you tried to kill yourself by jumping off a bridge. I knew I had.

In the afternoon, when everyone had had a nap, a Southerly Buster blew in and a cooling calm descended on the land. The trees, however, were screaming like Odysseus's sirens.

His back well doused in TCP lotion, Uncle James was busy setting up the barbecue with Dad and slurping down a couple of stubbies. Aunt Mary and Mum hung out our swimmers and towels and laughed off near-death experiences. The Hills Hoist spun like a tornado.

'Uncle James?'

'Yuuusss, John.'

I paused trying to find a better way of saying, 'Why are the trees screaming?' so that he wouldn't think that I was a total idiot. 'Why are the trees screaming?'

He skulled down the last of his beer. 'Cicadas.'

I nodded. Though, of course, I didn't know what a "cicadas" was. Was it a sort of animal, a disease that afflicted trees causing them to scream, the fifth letter of the Norwegian alphabet, or something you said when you finished your beer?

'Have you ever seen one?' he asked.

'A cicadas?' I shook my head.

Uncle James wandered over to the tree and returned, moments later, clutching a cicada by its wings.

I took one look at the thing and immediately leapt into a tree and did a bit of screaming of my own.

33

Going Home

Trish and I started school and Uncle James got Dad a job on his road gang. At that time entire suburbs such as Georges Hall didn't have the sewer connected. Outside dunnies were the order of the day, much to the delight of the squadrons of blowflies. The air resonated with their hum. The Australian salute (hand flapping wildly in front of your face like the Pope ascending in ecclesiastical ecstasy) was as much a national icon as football, meat pies, kangaroos and Holden cars. As a result there was plenty of labouring work available—excavating roadsides, laying sewer pipes. Dad and Uncle James took as much overtime as they could handle, quite often working twelve hours a day, seven days a week, breaking their backs and having their skins seared off by the sun—all so that people could crap indoors. Their work ethic made an enormous impact on me, so that even now as I type these words in my backyard hammock, I find myself overcome with a tremendous sense of guilt and a strange urge to dig up the nature strip.

Like most Irishmen, Dad and Uncle James had the thirst and would often come roaring in from work after they'd stopped off for a quick pint or fifteen on the way home.

Around this time, Aunt Mary started clouting me. A fiery redhead with a fearsome temper and firm right hand, she adored Trish almost as much as she despised me. I couldn't think what it was that I'd done to raise her ire, but each time I tried to redress the situation and ingratiate my way into her affections, it only seemed to piss her off more and I would end up either rubbing my head, seeing stars, or tearing off up the backyard in search of a bramble patch while she came at me with a broom. Sitting in the kitchen surrounded by baking trays and flour, Trish was as ill-equipped to deal with our role reversal as I was.

Pretty soon my mere existence seemed to get on Aunt Mary's goat. Walking through the kitchen with shoes on. Walking through the kitchen without shoes on. Walking through the kitchen while she was baking a cake with Trish. Walking through the kitchen and looking at her in a funny way. Walking through the kitchen. Failing to understand her accent. Slurping my tea. Not putting the toilet seat down after I'd finished having a pee. Not putting the toilet seat up when I *was* having a pee. Peeing on the toilet seat irrespective of its position. Peeing too noisily. Being a useless good-for-nothing little shite. And so on—and *on*—were all cloutable offences. Offences I always mysteriously seemed to commit when Mum and Dad were out looking for houses, cars, or work. Finally, having been thumped on the back of the head for being English, I stormed off to my bedroom with tears streaming down my face. I wedged my bed against the door to prevent the auld witch from getting in to administer a follow-up clouting for wedging my bed against the door.

I wasn't used to being clouted by adults. Mum was big on threats but rarely followed them through. 'You'll be laughing on the other side of your face in a minute' and 'Clean up this bloody room or I'll knock you into next week'. Occasionally she would say one of those strange things that all English women of a certain age did, usually after Trish had told on me: 'Mum, John was lying on the lounge wearing his muddy school shoes again.' Mum would look at me and say, 'I'll lie on the lounge wearing his muddy school shoes again *him* if he isn't careful.' Just reaching for her slipper was enough to scatter us to the winds. If she had one of her heads or it was raining so we couldn't go out to play and Trish, Paul, and I started making a 'Bloody din!', she said we were getting on her wick, neck, nerves, or goat; and if we didn't bloody behave we ran the risk of being thumped, thrashed, thraped, slapped, thick-eared, or belted. If we *really* stepped out of line we would receive a terse, 'Just wait till your father gets home', which did not exactly strike the fear of God into us. Dad meted out punishment like Gandhi and would just as likely have gone on a hunger strike over our behaviour as raised his hand to us. I can only recall him smacking me once as a child. I promptly pulled a Pugsley Porksworth and jettisoned the contents of my bladder like a garden hose that hasn't been weighed down with a brick. A rather effective defence strategy, seeing that he never laid a finger on me again.

Now, however, I was being clouted daily for nothing and I didn't know what to do about it. I slumped onto my bed and began composing a mental list:

Reasons to Go:
- Paper boys
- Houses only have downstairs
- Screen-doors go *click-clack*
- Clotheslines spin when you turn the handle
- The trees scream
- Cicadas
- Flies up your nose
- Flies in your mouth
- Flies in your ear
- Outside dunnys
- Bindiis
- Vegemite

- Sharks bite you on the bum when you are on the toilet (Perth)
- Sharks chomp off your arms when you try to kill yourself by jumping off a bridge (Georges Hall)
- Beaches try to cart your mum off to New Zealand
- Aunties clout you for walking through the kitchen with your shoes on
- Aunties clout you for walking through the kitchen without your shoes on
- Aunties clout you for walking through the kitchen while they are baking cakes with your sister
- Aunties clout you for walking through the kitchen and looking at them in a funny way
- Aunties clout you for walking through the kitchen
- Aunties clout you for failing to understand their accent
- Aunties clout you for slurping your tea
- Aunties clout you for not putting the toilet seat down after you have a pee
- Aunties clout you for not putting the toilet seat up when you are having a pee
- Aunties clout you for peeing on the toilet seat irrespective of its position
- Aunties clout you for peeing too noisily
- Aunties clout you for being a useless good-for-nothing little shite
- Aunties clout you for being English

Reasons to Stay:
- There's a kid in my class who can burp the national anthem

Ignoring the banging on the door in Irish, I crawled out of bed and started to pack my little duffle bag.

'John, John,' whispered Trish through the door a short while later. 'Let me in.'

Not by the hair of my chinny, chin, chin. Not while the big, bad Irish wolfhound was outside, at any rate.

'It's okay,' said Trish. 'Aunt Mary's out'back.'

I pulled back the bed a bit so that Trish could squeeze in.

She looked at my duffle bag. 'What are you doing?'

'I'm going home.'

'Where to?'

'Maltby,' I snivelled. 'I hate it here!'

'But who will you stay with?'

'Auntie Margaret and Uncle Harry. Or Auntie Dympna and Uncle Albert. They'd never clout me for being English. They *are* English.'

'Not Auntie Dympna. *She's* Irish.'

'Yeah, but she wouldn't clout me for it, would she? Or she'd be clouting Uncle Albert the entire time.'

'Why don't you just tell Mum and Dad?' said Trish.

'I can't,' I sniffed.

'Why not?'

'Because we'd have to go back and live in that shed

and Dad would have to work in the steelworks. And we'd have to eat fruit off the sand, and I don't even like fruit.'

'What are you talking about?'

'Doesn't matter.'

I tied up my duffle bag. It contained my pyjamas, coat, snorkel, goggles, and a shoehorn.

'How will you get there?'

'I'm going to catch the *Achille Lauro*. It won't be full going back. I'll live in our wardrobe if I have to. Giovanni will let me in.'

'The *Achille Lauro* will have gone by now.'

'All right then, I'll fly.'

Trish stared at me with her hands on hips. 'And *how* will you get to the airport.'

'Oh I don't know! I'll follow the planes or something. Stop compicat . . . stop complucat . . . stop campulating . . . *shut up!*'

'Why don't you just stay out of her way?'

That was unfair. I was practically invisible as it was. If I tried to stay out of her way any harder I'd be forced to strip back to my molecules.

'Wait there!' ordered Trish.

She squeezed her way out of the room. What followed sounded suspiciously like half a dozen cats arguing in a sack. A couple of minutes later she squeezed her way back into the room and tipped up my duffle bag. 'Aunt Mary said she's not going to hit you anymore.'

'Why not?'

'Because I told her if she hit you again *I'd* hit her back.'

'What did she say?'

'She said she was sorry.' Perhaps Aunt Mary was aware of Trish's reputation around the cutlery drawer and Mum's sewing kit. 'She said that she had no right hitting you in the first place.'

I'd often wondered what would happen if Trish ever decided to use her powers for good instead of evil.

'She said to go outside and play and she'd make you a nice cup of tea and give you a slice of cake.'

With the beast in the bramble patch now in my corner, I stamped through the kitchen, pausing only to poke my tongue out at Aunt Mary's back. Then I stomped out through the *click-clack* screen-door and peed on the dunny seat, being extra noisy about it. I then spent the rest of the afternoon climbing the screaming trees and keeping a lookout for planes that I might be forced to follow in the future.

34

'I've Been Eating Paste'

After about two months we finally found a place of our own. As we packed the last of our belongings into the ute that Dad had hired for the occasion, I was positive I could hear an Irish jig coming from inside Uncle James and Aunt Mary's house.

Until we moved out of their place we'd been part of the Irish community. This consisted of turning up to a different house every Friday night with a couple of bottles of beer, some sausages and a bowl of potato salad, and listening while the men clinked glasses and sang protest songs about the working conditions in New York. Occasionally a man with an accordion would turn up and take centre stage until he could be persuaded to go away again.

Now we were on our own.

Our new home was a small weatherboard house in Erica Crescent, just off Bankstown Airport. Elsewhere in the western suburbs of Sydney you would find backyards strewn with old engine parts and rusted car bodies. In Georges Hall a number of the backyards had plane wrecks in them, some of which had clearly come off second best in a dispute over the laws of gravity. One of the houses across Birdwood Reserve contained the fuselage of an abandoned McDonnell Douglas DC3. I think the owners had moved out of the house and into the plane. I used to imagine the service trolley being wheeled up the aisle at mealtimes.

It all seemed so exciting and new. I'd never lived in a plane before. I wondered what it would be like. Then again, I'd never lived in a cul-de-sac before either. The possibilities seemed endless. Or at any rate the chances of being run over were severely diminished, albeit at the increased risk of having an aircraft plummet into your living room. Aside from that, things were definitely look-ing up. Aunt Mary had stopped clouting me and, perhaps to celebrate our departure, had made library bags for Trish and me to take to school. So I decided to stay in Australia—for a while, at least.

Our new next-door neighbours were a worried look-ing man and his snooty wife. The worried looking man turned out to be a professor of something incredibly clever. He was startlingly thin and loped along like a giraffe caught in a gale, though we didn't see much of him because he and his beard were permanently buried under a pile of books in his study. The rumour in the street was that he was trying to sticky tape an atom back together and that he would kill us all in the process.

According to Mum, the professor's wife was born with a silver spoon up her arse. She wore long, flowing gowns that would get caught in her car door and flap along outside like Batman's cape.

Looking out of her kitchen window one evening, she spotted me having a pee against the side fence. I was too scared to use the outside dunny in case a redback spider or Trish was lurking inside.

'You shouldn't be doing that,' she intoned while holding her pinkie finger perpendicular to the horizon.

I tapped the little fireman and pulled up my pants. '*You* shouldn't be looking.'

My first day at Georges Hall Primary School the previous month hadn't exactly been a roaring success. My new teacher had made me stand up in front of the class and introduce myself. I was only about half a sentence into my life story when kids collapsed out of their chairs and flailed about on the ground, kicking their legs in the air like upturned sea-turtles. Even the teacher was snorting like a Colombian airport beagle as she told me to resume my seat and that we'd have to try again some other time.

At lunchtime I sat by myself to eat my Vegemite sandwiches. I watched dumbstruck as an enormous stick crawled out of a tree, along the ground, and walked up some surprised kid's leg. That was another couple of things I'd have to add to my list: kids and teachers laughed at your Yorkshire accent, and some of the sticks walked up your leg. And just what was this black shite on my sandwiches, anyway?

When you're six going on seven, if you tell your friends that you want to be a pilot or a brain surgeon they'll probably think that's okay if you've got somewhere you need to go or you have a sore head or something. It means very little. But if you can burp the national anthem, well, the world is your oyster. I might have spent the rest of my time at Georges Hall Primary eating lunch alone, feeling miserable for myself and keeping an alert karate pose on lookout for those sticks that walked up your leg, but my luck changed when I was given a seat next to the class lunatic. My stock improved immeasurably.

I'd only been there a week when we were given a maths test. I scored a perfect mark and was promptly shuffled up into the top class and left the snorting sea-turtles behind.

'Welcome, John,' said my new teacher, Mrs Henuke. 'It's nice to have you join us. What *is* that smell?' I reeled for a moment, thinking that she was having a go at me. But then I realised she was referring to the repugnant reek that filled the classroom. The students agreed that there was a dreadful pong about, but they didn't know where it came from. One of the boys suggested that it probably emanated from the trousers of David Dawkins. But he was told to be quiet *this instant!*

I was introduced to my new classmates but it was free-play time and they weren't really interested. Rather than laugh at my accent, they ignored me completely. Mrs Henuke gave me a special pencil with my name on it and told me to take the desk next to David Dawkins.

I wandered over to the only spare seat in the room. The intensity of the pong increased with each step I took.

'Hello,' I said to my new neighbour. 'My name's John. I've just moved here from England.'

David Dawkins looked up from whatever it was he was doing—rolling snotballs, as far as I could tell.

'I've been eating paste,' he said, gazing into an alternative reality.

I sat down at my desk. 'What did you say?'

He returned to his snotballs, which were quite large. 'I've been eating paste. Do you want some?'

'Er—no thanks.'

'I had a pet hamster,' he continued. 'It died about two weeks ago. I was going to have a funeral for it but I decided to keep it in my pencil case instead. Want to have a look?'

Before I had the chance to scream 'No!' he unzipped the dead rodent's coffin. The stench shot up my nose and pierced the back of my brain like a wayward javelin at a school athletic carnival.

Peering into the depths of David Dawkins's pencil

case, I could clearly see the outline of a decomposing rat. I think he'd shoved a pencil up its bum and was using it as a sort of decorative gonk.

'That's not a hamster. It's a rat!' I was a big fan of *Tales of the Riverbank* so I knew my stuff.

'Sssshhhh!' he hissed like a cornered snake. 'He's a rat, but he thinks he's a hamster. He might hear you.'

'But it's dead.'

'His ghost might hear you, then.'

Unfortunately no one else in the class knew just how insane David Dawkins was—it would be months before he climbed onto the roof of the administration block and peed on the headmaster. But prior to that he did have a bit of playground cred because he could burp the national anthem.

No one at school in Maltby could burp *God Save the Queen* as far as I could remember. Pugsley Porksworth had once tried to fart *Land of Hope and Glory*, but had ended up with some serious follow-through that meant he had to go home for a change of clothes.

David Dawkins might have been on the top branch of the deranged tree, but he had plenty of company up there with him. I don't know if it was a reflection on the school, the diet at the time, or our proximity to so much aviation fuel, but the playground at Georges Hall Public seemed to have a disproportionate number of unhinged kids hurtling about it. When Mrs Henuke asked us what we wanted to be when we grew up, one or two of the boys and several girls said that they wanted to be horses. I'd heard strange snorting and snuffling sounds in the cloakroom before, but I just thought one of them had a cold.

Aside from the group equine fantasy, a considerable number of boys clearly had plans to become aeroplanes. At lunch they would go tearing around the playground with their arms outstretched and their tongues vibrating faster than a humming bird's wings as they simulated a diving Spitfire. All but one of them (Robbie Megson wanted to be a commercial airliner) had their hearts set on being fighter jets. And you knew this because when they weren't engaged in energetic dogfights with each other, strafing the horses, or performing intricate loop-the-loops outside the girls' toilets, they would get involved in side skirmishes with the joy flights lifting off from Bankstown Airport.

David Dawkins was the undoubted leader of the lunatics, though. Evidently he had his hopes pinned on becoming the Hindenberg, because he certainly produced enough noxious gas to lift him into the stratosphere.

When he wasn't eating twigs, rocks, dirt or bits of himself, he would charge about the playground like the Looney Toons Tasmanian Devil. Occasionally he would stop to land a mule-kick on some unsuspecting girl, before making off with her lunch, skipping rope, handball or shoe. When the bell rang for the end of lunch, he would flatly refuse to come inside. If a teacher tried to force him back to class he would make a sound like a donkey being scalded.

When the police, the fire brigade, the television news crew and the still-dripping headmaster finally coaxed him down from the roof of the administration block that fateful day, he was led quietly away in his Hannibal Lector muzzle, never to return.

Some of the kids in class said that he'd been carted off to a boys' home. If Mrs Henuke knew what had happened to him, she wasn't letting on. I like to think that he just exploded. He would have wanted it that way.

Grandma Kennedy and Big Tom took advantage of the family reunion scheme and joined us in Georges Hall. Uncle Tim had emigrated the year before us and was living up in the blazing north of Western Australia, carving out a living in the open-cut mines in and around Port Hedland.

When Grandma and Big Tom arrived, I had to give up my room and share with Trish. I didn't mind this too much because since the incident with Aunt Mary, Trish herself wasn't threatening to kill me as often.

A great walker, Big Tom resumed his long treks and would spend his days striding stoutly along the Georges River and making curious forays into Bankstown Airport. Sometimes he would take Trish and me with him, promising us a thick ear if we complained that we'd gone too far and wanted to go home.

Like all old men, he enjoyed collecting "interesting" things on his treks and would arrive back home with tin cans, bits of string, copper wire, sheets of asbestos, or a dead goat.

With Grandma on hand to look after us kids, Mum found work in a cake shop in Bankstown. One of her regular customers was the mother of up-and-coming cricketer Jeff Thomson. It would be unethical of me to break the cake shop code of conduct by revealing how many pies, sausage rolls, cream buns and chocolate éclairs you needed to shove down your gob to become the fastest bowler on the planet. Though it did seem to be rather a lot.

35

Chickenzgutosleep

It seemed as though we'd just settled into life at Georges Hall when we were on our way again. Not back to Maltby, unfortunately, but to a brand new house in Toongabbie, a *sort of* historic suburb that had been one of the earliest outlying settlements of Sydney. The original settlers had built a railway station and a pub, caught the train to the pub and had pretty much left it at that. Now, however, with the rapid expansion of Sydney's suburban sprawl, chook pens and cow paddocks were giving way to housing estates.

I wasn't too upset about the prospect of moving again. Georges Hall had only ever felt temporary, our roots shallow ones. In fact my most vivid memory of Georges Hall is of spending an entire day waiting on our front veranda for the pool to be delivered.

Janice and Bert—the couple who lived the other side of us—had told us that our landlords had an above ground pool. Prior to heading off on their around

Australia odyssey, however, they'd packed it up and placed it in storage. They were worried that their prospective tenants might have been elderly, or at any rate not had any children, and that as a result their pool would fall into disuse and neglect. Janice and Bert gave us the landlord's phone number in Brisbane in case we wanted to get in touch and arrange to have the pool delivered.

I'd never been so excited in my life. I could learn how to swim. How to dive. How to make elaborate plunges over my handlebars once I'd crashed my scooter into the side of the pool. I would leap, Birdman like, off the dunny roof and leave a squadron of startled blowflies in my wake. I would learn how to breathe underwater and be the envy of my friends, and be known far and wide as the boy who could breathe underwater. I would... I would... I would do such *things*.

The following Saturday I leapt out of bed so I could see the pool arriving. First, though, I had to get through the morning cartoons. My favourite was about a mutated man/budgerigar called Birdman. Half bird, half man, Birdman had all the advantages of being a man, plus the incalculable bonus of being able to flap up into the clouds and shit on passers-by, more or less at random. I wanted desperately to be a birdman—or birdboy, at least. I would practise jumping off the back veranda, flapping my flippers like a demented cockatoo. The sneers from next door that accompanied each inelegant

collision with the ground made me even more determined to succeed. And when I did, I fully intended to
pee on the stuck-up cow's kitchen window from on high.

At the end of each episode, Birdman would soar off
into the sunset and bellow, 'BIRD*MAN*!' at the top of
his voice, which was a bit odd. It would be like me hovering over the dunny roof with my flippers and shouting,
'JOHN!'

When Birdman had flapped off for another week, I
quickly changed and dragged a kitchen chair out to the
front veranda to start waiting for the pool.

Each time a car turned into our street I jumped up,
eyes as wide and bright as beach balls and yelled, 'It's
here! It's here!' As soon as I saw that the car belonged
to one of our neighbours, or was anyway not pool-
related, I collapsed onto the floor of the veranda like a
zebra under a pride of lions in one of those nature shows
that my grandma liked to watch.

I waited out there the whole day and well into the
evening. My enthusiasm only slightly diminished by the
fact that not only had Mum and Dad failed to phone
the landlord, they had never intended to because we
were moving.

So we covered the wagon and headed west.

Although we'd often visited our house as it was being
built, we all wanted to be involved in the first move.
We must have looked remarkably like the Clampetts
heading to Beverly Hills as our flatbed truck trundled

along Woodville Road—a stretch of such breathtaking ugliness that you would need to visit a war zone to find its equal.

Grandma sat up front in the cabin with Mum, Dad and Paul, while Trish, Big Tom, the cat and I were behind with the furniture—sort of human octopus straps. I can't remember seeing much of Trish on that maiden trip. I think she was hiding in one of the wardrobes.

Halfway there, the cat managed to escape from its basket. It spent the rest of the journey crouched on top of Mum's dressing table and growling strangely. I suppose to fully appreciate its terror you would need to experience the unique sensation of being a cat hurtling along Woodville Road on top of a dressing table that was travelling at over sixty kilometres an hour.

Big Tom really looked the part, though, relaxing in one of the armchairs and smoking his pipe. He was like Hemingway hanging off the back of a big game trawler off the coast of Cuba. If only he'd thought to dangle his fishing rod over the tailgate, the picture would have been complete.

'Look,' he said. 'There's fourteen of them in there. Fourteen! The daft sods. That's a new record.' He pointed the smouldering wet end of his pipe at one of the passing cars.

A popular game among Italian migrants in the seventies was to see how many family members you could cram into your car, which was usually, for some reason, a white Valiant.

Unfortunately I couldn't have a laugh with him at the way the Italians travelled. I was too busy trying to hold down the cat, which was making a desperate bid for freedom at each set of traffic lights we came to. I was also wary in case Trish suddenly decided to leap out of the wardrobe and claw me half to death.

The house was so new that it still smelled of varnish and the workmen's cigarettes. It also made strange creaking and cracking sounds throughout the night. Mum said it was the house settling. It took a long time to settle, though, because it was still creaking and cracking twenty years later, and is probably still at it now.

Dad and Big Tom made several more trips to fetch the remainder of our stuff, while the rest of us alternated between packing things away, making beds, and attempting to coax the cat down from its tree.

Later that night, as dusk crept silently east across the Nullarbor Plain, I was woken by a bloodcurdling scream.

I pulled the covers up over my eyes and prayed to God to save us from the salivating monster outside our window, or, failing that, convince it to eat Trish first so that I could escape.

I'd just about nodded off when another scream rang out into the night.

'Trish,' I whispered as softly as I could so that I

wouldn't attract the monster's attention. 'Trish! What was *that*?'

'Chickens,' she said. 'Now go to sleep.'

Because I was two years younger than Trish, I was losing my Yorkshire accent and becoming an Aussie much more quickly than she was. So what she actually said and what I heard were separated by the equator and several time zones.

I lay there terrified (a pair of eyeballs and a sheet) wondering what on earth "chickenzgutosleep" were and why Mum and Dad weren't coming in to rescue us from these dangerous chickenzgutosleep? Perhaps they'd already been eaten.

It wasn't until the following morning when Mum said, 'Did you hear that racket them roosters were making last night?' that the mystery was cleared up.

Over the next couple of months, until we became accustomed to the racket, we got to know the roosters' sleep patterns quite well. You could set your clock by them—provided that it wasn't your alarm clock.

At some point in the night—usually around 10.23—our resident rooster would suddenly get the idea that it was dawn. He would start screeching his thoughts on the subject, which mostly involved a long monologue about how great it was to be poultry and therefore excluded from having to get up and go to work, unlike some that he could mention.

Then every rooster within a one-kilometre radius

would join in the ruckus. Whether the others were agreeing with our rooster, or telling him to shut his bloody beak because it was only 10.23, I really couldn't say. The combined effect, however, was like a drunken giraffe falling headfirst into the brass section of the Darwin Symphony Orchestra in cyclone season.

Just when you thought that the roosters had gone completely insane (or you had), suddenly all would be silent. It stayed that way just long enough for you to either drop off to sleep, or pack your shotgun away. Five seconds later and they'd be at it again.

Sleeping with your head buried under your pillow offered some relief, as long as you were stone deaf to begin with. Otherwise there was no escaping the racket, which continued throughout the night, with brief interludes that ranged from two hours to two minutes long.

I'd always been led to believe that roosters only crowed at dawn. As it happens dawn was, paradoxically, the one time you could guarantee peace and quiet. Understandable, really, given that the roosters had been up half the night anticipating its arrival. When it finally did turn up, they were suddenly too exhausted to give a toss.

So dawn generally broke to an eerie silence.

When I look back at my childhood in Toongabbie I wonder how I survived at all ... Sorry; wrong book. The thing I miss most from those days is, oddly enough, that chaos in the night. There's nothing like being snug and warm in your bed, hearing the cocks crow and knowing you still have anything from two to nine hours left to sleep in.

Whatever you do, do not leave this planet until you've experienced this. It's strangely alluring.

36

Fascists in Beanies, Percussion Music and School Milk

Our new next-door neighbours were Dave and Maureen Luck, who were migrants from England too. They had three boys: Michael, who was the same age as me, and Graeme and Alan, who were a bit younger. They also had a baby daughter called Julie. Dave, who we later nicknamed The Major (which was daft really because it wasn't a naval rank) was an NCO (non-commissioned officer) in the Australian Navy.

The day we arrived, Michael and Graeme were having a terrific time swinging their cat around by its tail as if they were competing in the hammer throw. I had never seen a more resigned looking cat in my life. I think it had even fallen asleep as it went sailing through the air for the umpteenth time. I would have said something to them, only I was busy trying to poke my own cat down from its tree with a broom.

Michael and I became instant friends, mostly because our mothers insisted on it. Then he introduced me to two other boys about our age who lived in the same street. They were Darryl Nelson, who—and I still don't know why—insisted on calling himself Smackamoo, and Tony O'Neil, who Darryl called Tosh, although he was English rather than Welsh.

Our house and the Lucks' backed onto the Marist Fathers' Seminary. Our street, Hurley Street, was apparently named after one of its former priests. Father Hurley (or so the rumour went) had apparently been decapitated by someone who was less than pleased to see him. Whether this was true or not there *was* a small graveyard in the Marist Fathers where Father Hurley was buried.

Showing scant regard for consecrated ground, Michael, Darryl, Tony, another boy called Shane Easson and I would go and read the headstones of these dead priests and make up stories about what had happened to them. One day Darryl decided that the only way to tell whether Father Hurley had been decapitated or not was to dig him up. Fortunately the insane Afghan hound that roamed the seminary grounds like a hairy ghost scattered us shortly after we began excavating.

Although I was rarely in trouble with my parents, I

think I might have taken a bit of a hiding had I returned home with the severed head of a priest.

On one of my first weekends in Toongabbie, Michael Luck, Darryl Nelson and I had a sleepover at Tony O'Neil's house. Part way through the night we were woken by strange snorting and snuffling sounds outside his bedroom window. We all assumed that it was Tony's older brother Terry up to no good. With a 'Cut it out, Terry!' Michael crawled out of his sleeping bag and flung open Tony's curtains. Peering in through the window from the vacant lot next door was a large horse. Michael went into such a state of shock that he had to be escorted home by Tony's father. I don't think he ever fully recovered.

Another English couple who lived in our street were Norm and Irene Ralph. Irene was an elegant woman and walked with her head erect in a slightly aloof manner that seemed to say, 'I might work in a factory, but I do it with style.' She was sheer class. Mum hated her on sight.

Yorkshire people are notorious for their inverted snobbery, 'There may have been thirty-six of us living in a shed at bottom of t'slag heap, but we knew our place in t'world and it were better than been a bloody chinless toff.'

When Irene Ralph walked past our house on her way to work each morning, Mum used to call us all over to the front window. 'Look at that stuck up bloody cow!

Who does she think she is? If her nose gets any higher it'll start bleeding.'

A few weeks later Mum started work at the same factory Irene worked at and they became best friends and have remained so to this day.

Norm Ralph was a huge man with a terrific sense of humour. He looked like Mr Brady out of *The Brady Bunch* except, being from Portsmouth, he talked out the side of his mouth. He was the sort of guy you would choose for an uncle. He was also a wonderful storyteller.

The Ralphs hadn't been in Australia all that long when Norm was driving down the street in his car. Hearing a strange noise he pulled over and lifted up the bonnet. He couldn't find the source, climbed back in and carried on. A short while later the noise started up again. So he pulled over a second time but couldn't find anything wrong with the engine. He drove on, cautious and confused—another victim of the screaming trees.

My new teacher at Toongabbie Public School was Mrs Thrower, a formidable English woman who was always dressed in black. She wore long flowing frocks that reached the floor and would have looked more at home in a Charles Dickens novel than on the blunt end of a piece of chalk that could become a projectile at the drop of a word or fart. Rumour had it that Mrs Thrower kept bats up her frocks, though what was in it for the bats I couldn't say.

On rainy days she would while away the afternoon

by telling us gripping tales of Luftwaffe raids over London. Given the number of bombs the German pilots dropped on her house, they had apparently taken a marked disliking to her.

Despite her caring nature, Mrs Thrower was by no means a pushover—her smacking technique was the stuff of legend. If you stepped out of line, were involved in a fight, or looked like turning into a paste-eater, Mrs Thrower would lift up the leg of your shorts to reveal most of your upper leg and a good deal of pristine white buttock as well. Meanwhile her other hand would have commenced its massive back swing. At the moment of impact, time seemed to stand still and you found yourself at one with the universe. You knew what it was to be a flower, a bee, or a frog on a lily pad. You understood what it meant to be an albatross far out at sea or a lemming on a cliff. Philosophers counted as you danced on the pinhead with your fairy brothers and sisters. You had reached nirvana. Then the echo of the enormous *thwack* rebounded off the back wall and the searing pain hit you like a fully laden locomotive. You literally had to bite your lip to stop from howling. And although you were now able to resume your seat, it was rather difficult to do so with one of your arse cheeks on fire. You were desperate to go to the toilet and lower yourself onto one of those ice-cold seats. Unfortunately Mrs Thrower wouldn't let you out until play lunch and, besides, the entrance to the toilets was usually guarded by a couple of fascists in beanies.

Around this time I discovered girls. Not in any physical way, but I found that I liked them—a lot.

It was actually quite a shock to learn that there were girls who didn't want to run you over, rip your teddy bear's head off, attack you with forks, knives and knitting needles, or tie you down and tickle your feet until you were ready to vomit.

Jasmine Robards and Annette Oakley were blonde, blue-eyed cherubic visions. I couldn't decide which of them I liked best, so I fell in love with both.

Being in love when you're eight years old means lots of chasing and name-calling and I don't suppose it's much different later on. At dinner one evening I let slip my feelings for Jasmine Robards. I was trying to write a poem about her but couldn't think of a word to rhyme with "Robards" other than "Bollards", which, even had it been a perfect rhyme, didn't seem right. Trish was on it in a flash, composing a little ditty of her own that went, 'If Jasmine Robards lived over the sea, What a great swimmer John would be.' Although I felt I was being unfaithful, I chose not to mention Annette Oakley, figuring that it would only stoke Trish's fire even more. And besides, all I could find to rhyme with Annette's last name was "Pokely".

During percussion music I would watch Jasmine and Annette *tinging* their triangles until I was fit to chime myself. Their heads would bob in time with Mrs Thrower's piano and I so desperately wanted—well, I didn't know what I wanted other than perhaps to yank their ponytails, then run away and hide.

So I became a fascist instead. It was much easier.

I would like to think that the headmistress, Mrs Nelson, chose me and David Griffiths to be the school's inaugural playground monitors because we had many fine leadership qualities and because we were mature and intelligent young men who could liaise between the teachers, the administration staff (the cleaners), and the student body. In reality, however, I think we were just standing the straightest at assembly.

I would also like to be able to report that we handled our newfound authority with a maturity that belied our tender years. Tragically, though, we rather let the moment go to our heads and set about creating a totalitarian state. Attired in our storm trooper outfits (anoraks and beanies) we would arrest kids who'd committed crimes against the state, such as leaving the bubbler running too long before taking a drink, or having jumper sleeves rolled up, or, heaven forbid, looking at us in a manner that seemed to question our authority. The amazing thing was, though, that kids actually obeyed us.

'Hagan, I've warned you before about standing back from the trough. It eventually runs out, you know, and then there's a mess on the floor.'

'Shut up, Larkin!'

'What did you say?'

'Nuthin', Griffiths.' Hagan would then follow his steaming arc forwards until he was at a more acceptable distance from the urinal. If he didn't move quickly enough for our liking, we would kick his heels until he went sliding along the floor, painting his initials on the stainless steel wall as he did.

David and I would then leave but hide around the corner in case he took a step backwards. Hagan knew we were hiding around the corner, however, because that's the sort of thing we did, and as a regular flouter of the rules he was familiar with our policing methods. But because we knew that he knew we would be hiding around the corner, we could actually leave and get on with more serious law enforcing—like lecturing kindergarten kids because they looked like they might be thinking of throwing that rock—content in the knowledge that Hagan wouldn't take a step back because a) he knew we were hiding around the corner (even though we weren't) and b) he was fast running out of urine.

My only moment of triumph as a playground monitor came when I chased off a bunch of first graders who were teasing an Indian girl. Through some gross geographical error on their part, however, they were making North American Indian hollers as they rode their imaginary horses around her. I shooed them off and then came back to see if she was okay. I wiped her tears and offered her half my Tim-Tam. She looked up at me

and smiled and immediately joined Jasmine Robards and
Annette Oakley on my list. Her smile was so drop-dead
gorgeous that I had to physically restrain myself from
yanking her ponytail, running off and hiding, and
perhaps making a few hollering sounds of my own.

At the end of my tenure (one week) I returned to
civilian life just in time to be dealt the first real disappointment of my life.

Our school was having its annual Easter hat parade.
However, because it was my first year at Toongabbie
Public, and because we didn't go in for such pagan rituals in Maltby, I didn't really know what was involved,
and, more to the point, the note detailing the parade
that I had in my bag had been made indecipherable by
one of my squashed and decaying bananas.

The night before the parade I tried to explain it to
Mum as well as I could, but because it was her first
Easter hat parade too, she was as much in the dark as
I was.

'Is there a note?'

Yes. 'No.'

'Well what do you have to do?'

'Wear a hat.'

'What sort of hat?'

'An Easter hat.'

'Easter hat? What Easter hat?'

I shrugged. 'I don't know.'

'What's an Easter hat when it's at home?'

'Jesus wore a crown of thorns at Easter,' said Grandma.

'He can't wear a crown of bloody thorns to school, Mam.'

'It was good enough for Our Lord,' replied Grandma, but Mum ignored her.

'You don't own a hat,' said Mum.

'Can't we make one?'

'Well we could have if you'd told me sooner.'

I shrugged.

'You'll have to wear one of your grandad's hats, then.'

I gulped, but said nothing.

Big Tom had reached the age when it was indecent to be seen out of doors without a hat. This was partly due to custom, but mostly to the fact that he insisted on cutting his own hair with whatever he could get his hands on—scissors, electric knives, hedge trimmers— and with the sort of results you can only imagine. The hat Mum chose for me was a red and black checked stetson with (would you believe) a feather in its band. She realised that this didn't quite capture the spirit of the occasion, so she stuck a small hand-written note on the brim that read "Happy Easter".

It was only when we lined up for judging the next day that I understood how important it was for you to take notes home from school.

The kid on my left turned and looked at my stetson and gave a hollow laugh. Actually it was quite difficult for him to turn, because he had a birdcage on his head. It wasn't just a small budgie cage either, but one that was big enough to house a squadron of pterodactyls in mating season. There were several largish birds roosting in that hat, and the floor of it was strewn with scores of brightly coloured oversized Easter eggs.

The kid on my other side had really gone to town— or his mother had. He was adorned in a medieval castle, complete with moat and fully operational drawbridge. There were even figures with guns peering out through the ramparts. And although I was fairly certain that cowboys didn't live in medieval castles, I was equally certain that the judges would ignore the anachronism.

I stood there feeling totally miserable in Big Tom's stetson, being laughed at by one kid with a birdcage on his head and another with a medieval castle on his. If only I'd known about irony at the time.

When the judging was over I didn't get an honorary mention. I didn't even get an Easter egg.

I trudged home with my tail between my legs and Big Tom's stetson stuffed in my bag.

No matter how cold it was outside, school milk always arrived warm, as if Roland Roundbutt had been storing the entire crate in his trousers. If that wasn't bad enough, school milk always had those nasty chunky bits of cream on top that you had to dig through with a pencil if you wanted to get to the milk below. Some of the braver or more stupid kids would give their bottles a thorough shaking and, long after the milk monitors had left with their crate of empties, you would see them on the benches, still chewing the disgusting residue. Even when I managed to keep mine down, the drama was usually just beginning. Rather than being able to concentrate on what would happen if a train left Town Hall at 3.00 pm and another left Katoomba at 3.10 pm with no sandwiches in the buffet car (was it me, or did teachers have a perverse fascination with train time-tables?) I would sit there and feel the milk weighing heavily on my stomach, soaking up my toasted soldiers and breaking down my boiled egg before the long cur-dling process started. Some of the kids in my class, the righteous little shits, actually enjoyed morning milk. They would sit there comparing their milk moustaches until I was fit to vomit on them. Then someone would let fly with a milk burp, the dank, stale odour of which would take ages to disperse.

I had to do something. I couldn't take much more. So I became a milk monitor because I found a loop-hole in the system.

Although morning milk was compulsory, I had noticed that the only kids whose milk intake was *not* monitored were the milk monitors themselves. It was the milk monitors' job to deliver the crates to each class and then return the empties and stack them in the brick bunker at the school gate, ready for the milkman the following morning. Becoming a milk monitor, even though there wasn't an actual vacancy, was a stroke of genius on my part. Not actually doing a scrap of work during my time as milk monitor was simply inspired. The other boys all had their regular partners with whom they carried the crates to each class. I was more than happy to loaf around by the collection point doing nothing but dream of pulling Jasmine Robards', Annette Oakley's and Indira Narayan's ponytails, then running off and hiding. If a teacher or the headmistress happened along I would attempt to look busy by pointing at crates, barking out nonsensical commands to the other milk monitors, or, if worse came to worst, stacking an empty.

The big kids at school always seemed to have an equally big sounding name: Dominic Ovalchin, Stephanella Largebuns, or something equally improbable. As owners often take on the appearance of their dogs or vice versa, I was working on the theory that people started to look like their names. My own name, said rapidly, sounded like a gate banging in the wind, which even now seems about right.

The only time when it was good to be the big kid at school was during percussion music, because it was the big kid who generally got to bang the big bass drum.

Mrs Thrower would be playing Bach, Mozart, or some old English pastoral tune about dukes with a lot of time on their hands, on the piano to try and accompany the utter cacophony we created with our percussion instruments. The girls would be going *ting, ting, ting* on their triangles, while we boys would be *thwacka, thwacka, thwacking* our castanets. The paste-eater would be trusted with the cymbals and he would, at some point during the song, try to eat them. Meanwhile Roland Roundbutt would be beating the living daylights out of his bass drum for all he was worth, totally out of time.

Ting ting ting. Thwacka thwacka thwacka. Ting. Thwacka. Ting. Crash. Ting. Boom. Thwacka. Boom. Boom. Boom.

'Come on, Roundbutt, keep up.'

'Shut up, Hagan!'

'Be quiet, you two. And again. And a one and two. And a one and two. And a one and two and three.'

Ting ting ting. Thwacka thwacka thwacka. Ting. Thwacka. Ting. Crash. Ting. Thwacka. Boom. Boom. Boom.

'The grand old Duke of York.'

Ting ting ting. Thwacka thwacka thwacka. Ting. Thwacka. Ting. Crash. Ting. Thwacka. Boom. Boom. Boom.

'He had ten thousand men.'

Ting ting ting. Thwacka thwacka thwacka. Ting. Thwacka. Ting. Crash. Ting. Thwacka. Boom. Boom. Boom.

'He marched them up to the top of the hill.'

Ting ting ting. Thwacka thwacka thwacka. Ting. Thwacka. Ting. Crash. Ting. Thwacka. Boom. Boom. Boom.

'And he marched them down again.'
Boom. Boom. Boom. Boom. Boom. Boom. Boom. Split.
'Er, sorry, Miss. The drum broke.'
'Roll up your pants, Roland.'
THWACK!

37

Death in the Suburbs

The following year, along with Michael Luck and David Griffiths, I made my holy communion and became a card-carrying member of the Catholic Church. During the build-up to the big event I would kneel in the pew and pray as hard as I could. I would screw up my eyes and clench my hands together really tightly so that the priest could almost see the prayers leaking out the top of my head. It was just as well that Father Shepherd *couldn't* see my prayers. My attention span for all things ecclesiastical meant that the prayer was immediately followed by the image of four girls from my class dancing naked around our Hills Hoist in a manner that would have disturbed the old priest in more ways than one.

Also making his holy communion at the same time was Phillip Kelly. The Kellys were a lovely family who lived next door but one to us. Theirs was an old house on a quarter-acre block that was brilliant for playing wars around. These wars of ours were post–Red Baron but pre–Phantom Agent and probably sat somewhere between the Third Reich and the Khmer Rouge as far as the accent of the dying soldier went.

The Kellys seemed to be from a different time; they were an archetypal 1940s family. Like the Sullivans without contraception. Phillip was the youngest, but he had older brothers and sisters too numerous to count. Just when you thought you had a handle on the number of Kellys about the place, a previously undiscovered sibling would emerge from a remote wing in their rabbit warren of a house.

Paul, the eldest, scared the living daylights out of me. A six-year-old John Wayne was one thing, but I'd never encountered a real cowboy before. Whenever Paul was out of the house, Phillip and I would sneak into his room, which was strictly off limits, and have a snoop around. Pictures of heaving stallions and fearsome bulls adorned his bedroom walls. He also kept an extensive collection of stuffed animals and dead snakes in jars. His room smelled mostly of denim, leather, fur, scale and, while I was in there, fear. I think he harboured dreams of becoming a professional rodeo rider and I'm sure he packed up and headed west just as soon as his education and father permitted it.

Shortly after Phillip and I had made our holy communion, Big Tom went into hospital for a check-up and never came out again.

I wandered out to the lounge room one morning

and found Trish bawling her eyes out on the lounge and Dad staring impassively ahead in his chair watching the morning news.

'What's up with Trish, Dad?'

Dad turned and looked over at me. 'Your grandad died last night.' Then he went back to the news.

It felt as though I'd been clouted with a sledge-hammer. My grandad couldn't be dead. Not Big Tom. He was too big. Too strong. Immortal. We'd visited him the night before and he seemed to be getting better. There had to be some mistake. What would happen to all his hats? What would happen to Grandma?

I wasn't that close to Big Tom, not like Trish and Paul were anyway, and not as close as I was to Grandma. I think he knew it, which was why, after the disastrous Easter hat parade with his stetson, he'd built me a billy-cart. It was so huge that Michael, Darryl, Tony, Phillip, Paul and I could all ride in it together.

Now he was gone and Trish was heaving those disturbing sobs. And in this whole awful mess the person I felt sorry for most of all was Dad. I knew he'd come from a fairly wealthy and austere family (by Irish standards anyway). But to be unable to comfort his daughter when she really needed comforting must have been awful. Trish just sat there alone on the lounge, her heart breaking into a million pieces, but Dad simply could not reach out to her.

I would have loved to hug her myself. To have wiped

away her tears and told her that everything was going to be okay, even though it wasn't. But what could I do? I was a Larkin.

So she just sat there rocking and crying and heaving as though she might never stop. It was her eleventh birthday.

38

Canberra Calling

With Big Tom gone, Grandma packed up her bucking bronco teacup and moved over to Western Australia to be with Uncle Tim, her youngest. So it was back to just the five of us again.

Trish scored Grandma and Big Tom's old room, whereas Paul and I moved into the back bedroom. I didn't mind this at all, because it meant I was closer to the roosters' racket over the back fence.

Shortly after Big Tom's funeral and before she headed west, I asked Grandma one of those odd questions that spring to kids' minds:

'What will happen at the end of the century, Grandma?' This was 1972. So you can see why it was on my mind.

Grandma put down her knitting and sat me on her knee. 'Well, we'll go into a new century.'

'What will it be called?'

Grandma smiled. 'It will be the year 2000.'

'Will Jesus come back?' I asked.

'Some people think so,' replied Grandma. 'But I don't know, me darling. We'll just have to wait and see, won't we?'

'Will I be alive?'

'Yes,' said Grandma, giving me a hug. 'You'll be in your mid-thirties.'

'Will you be alive?'

Grandma sighed and reached for her tea. 'No. I'll just miss it.'

She died in November 1999.

Before she left for Western Australia and Big Tom left for Heaven, I used to love lying in bed on Friday nights, listening to the muffled tv out in the lounge-room, where Grandma would be watching her favourite show *World at War*. I would drift off to sleep, content in the knowledge that there was no school the next day.

Instead I would walk up to Binnalong Oval for soccer and breathe in the curious mixture of Big Ben pies and the lime that was used for line marking. I loved it, but the truly great days were when I scored a goal. Watching the ball fly into the net was a beautiful sight and, like Mrs Thrower's smacking, time would stand still until it dawned on me what I had just done.

David Griffiths's grandmother was our number one fan. She'd made up a special Pendle Hill Tigers bracelet, coloured it with black and gold crepe paper and—I can still scarcely believe it—glued on half a ping-pong ball (on which she had painted a large eyeball). She called this contraption her magic eye.

The thing was, we never lost a single match when David Griffiths's grandmother watched us play, largely because the other team were scared witless of the strange woman walking up and down the sideline with a gigantic eyeball strapped to her wrist.

I'd never shared a room with Paul before—not with just the two of us, anyway—and it was an interesting experience because he was going through a rather strange phase. Not only did he sleep with one of his arms covering his mouth and nose (he was obsessed with the smell of fresh pyjamas), he also liked taking things to bed with him. Dogs, cats, new shoes, books, can openers, biscuit barrels, stuffed toys, non-stuffed toys, rocks, garden gnomes, hedge trimmers, cricket bats, stumps, beach umbrellas, cushions, photos, paintings, ornaments, teacups, tins of Milo, coat hangers had turned up in Paul's bed at one time or another—and often all at once.

One time Dad had brought home an industrial pump from work and tried to fix it out in his shed. It was a greasy, rusty old thing that Mum wouldn't allow in the house. But the following morning when Dad got up to go to work, he couldn't find it anywhere. At some point in the night, Paul had dragged it out of the shed and had taken it to bed with him.

I didn't worry too much about Paul's mental state,

because I was going through a few problems of my own. After seeing Big Tom's coffin being lowered into his grave I suddenly became terrified of dying. I was convinced that I would die in my sleep, be buried, and then miraculously recover but be unable to claw my way out of the coffin. I would sit up in bed with the light on, rocking back and forth, trying desperately to stay awake. On really awful nights when I could feel the coldness of the grave around me, I would wake Paul up and pay him to stop me from falling asleep. Paul would manage to stay up for a while and poke me with the Totem Tennis pole or garden rake that he'd been sleeping with, whenever I dozed off. But soon he would be nodding off himself and in the end be quite happy to forfeit the million dollars that I'd promised him if he could keep me up the entire night.

Quite often when Paul had drifted back to sleep with his whipper-snipper, hubcap or fence paling, I would go and stand by the window and stare out at the night—perhaps hoping to catch a glimpse of Father Hurley's headless ghost wafting through the Marist Fathers'. I could see by the glow on the grass outside that Trish had her light on, too. I didn't learn until many years later that she was going through the nightly horror of trying to stay awake in case she found herself waking up in a sealed coffin too.

On the weekends as soon as Mum and Dad had gone to bed, Trish and I would sneak out of our bedrooms and watch corny old black and white British films in an effort to stay awake. If Mum and Dad were out at a party and Trish was babysitting us for a laugh, she would wake Paul up and get him ready for school. The poor little guy would be sitting there on the lounge, at midnight half dazed, with a bowl of Coco Pops and a packed lunch, wondering when the cartoons were coming on.

Through friends of ours from Maltby, who were now living in New Zealand, Mum and Dad became friendly with an older couple who lived in Canberra. So every couple of months or so, we would all pile into the car for the dreaded haul down the Hume Highway to Canberra, which, due to the state of the road at the time, was a lot further away than it is now. And both Mum and Dad were on a sixty-a-day habit. So how the three of us managed to survive the journey without being asphyxiated in the back remains a mystery.

Not that I minded visiting Uncle Peter and Aunty Joan—they were great. Uncle Peter would give us five dollars each, just for turning up; but despite the obvious economic advantages to be had by moving there permanently, Trish and I protested long, loud and successfully when Mum and Dad started to talk about it. We'd had enough of moving. Trish would miss her friends. I would miss the roosters.

Despite *our* victory, Paul did much better out of these trips than we did. The little trouser-snake could really trade on cute. Mum always insisted on him taking his guitar and he would belt out thrash-metal, Irish folk songs until Uncle Peter paid him to stop. Trish's encyclopaedic knowledge of contemporary music and my ability to juggle a soccer ball on my head a couple of thousand times also impressed Uncle Peter, but not enough for him to go for his wallet again.

The trip that now takes three and a half-hours would take us almost six, because the car always looked as if it was about to break up.

The car, a Marina, was brand new when we bought it, but I'm sure Mum and Dad would have had second thoughts had they known it would tremble like a re-entering Apollo spacecraft whenever they tried to take it over eighty kilometres an hour. The Leyland organisation had abandoned its interest in the South-East Asian market not long after we bought the Marina, but occasionally a P76 would still turn up (lugging behind it the sort of robust boot that could quite comfortably contain another P76) much to the amusement of passers-by.

The Marina was fitted with vinyl seats which, in summer, would fix themselves to your skin and in winter plummet to a level that would have seen Scott making note in his diary if he'd owned a Marina and gone to the trouble of transporting it to the Antarctic: "Seats frozen solid. Too cold to even think. What's left of the food is in the boot, only we can't get it open. Sent

Oates out for a walk to find a crowbar. He may be some time."

The back seat had, or rather didn't have, doors, or windows that could be wound down. You gained access to it over the front seat in a complicated gymnastic manoeuvre that involved a one-and-a-half forward roll; there was a pike of sorts in there as well. So in the back seat, you were a captive audience—and, because air-conditioning was still an optional and expensive extra in the seventies, an extremely hot and bothered one at that. The fact that the front seat came with a mother who flatly refused to wind the window down any more than a finger width, because she'd been to Johnny's Hair Emporium in Toongabbie that morning, only increased the violence that erupted from time to time in the back.

Another glaring design flaw, probably not unique to Leyland, was that the engineers had failed to install ejector seats that would automatically activate if somebody started singing 'one hundred green bottles', or looked like they might be about to utter that gut-wrenching phrase, 'I spy...'

When we became really bored we would play crush. You had to fling yourself heavily to the left whenever the Marina went right and vice versa. Paul, the smallest by five years, would come off the worst in crush, which, considering the monetary rewards waiting for him in Canberra, pleased Trish and me no end.

We would play crush until Mum's teeth started to

grind and she looked like she might be thinking of going for her shoe, or Dad said, 'Will yis be quiet!' both of which worked immediately.

When it became so hot that everyone except Dad started drowsing, I would stick my spaghetti legs between Mum and Dad's seats to try and get comfortable. I think this probably annoyed Dad, though he never said. It certainly annoyed Trish. And when I fell asleep she would hit or scratch me and make it look like she'd struck out in her dream.

Whenever we invaded each other's space, the resulting fights would involve Trish's nails, my knees and Paul threatening to take off his Hush Puppies and shove them up our noses. In this regard we were pretty evenly matched.

Allegiances were forged and quickly broken as we fought to occupy the greatest number of vinyl upholstery panels, most of which were usually held by Trish. Whenever these pitch-battles escalated to hair-pulling and blood-drawing, Mum's hand would join us in the back, flapping around like a landed fish. Somehow she managed to do this while simultaneously smoking a cigarette, nodding off and reading a Catherine Cookson novel—and that was a skill the three of us never fully appreciated.

Actually Dad was the one who probably instigated a lot of these cloutings. One sideways glance from him would be enough for Mum to unleash the landed fish, once she'd finished the paragraph she was on. The amazing thing was, though, that she never connected, due to either a tragic lack or abundance of skill on her part; I was never sure. The ferocity of the strokes and deafening thud of hand careering against vinyl had a sobering effect on us. It wasn't so much what the hand had done in the past that brought us quickly into line; more a promise of what it might do in the future.

The only time one of us actually got hit was when, in a moment of madness, Mum totally lost the plot. It was a disgustingly hot day, the vinyl had begun to liquefy, and Mum either had one of her heads, had given up smoking for about the hundredth time, or had switched her allegiance to Fay Weldon. Whatever the reason, the debate over whether my favourite groups Smokie and Racey were a patch on David Essex and Suzie Quatro had turned hostile and, in a totally unprecedented move, at least as far as the car was concerned, Mum went for her shoe.

If it hadn't been so hot, things might have turned out differently, but the shoe, which on a colder day would have been strapped to her foot, was lying on the floor and available for immediate deployment. This went against all standard operating procedures. At home, the use of her shoe and other foreign objects was fully expected; and there was many a time her right shoe (she was left handed) went sailing over our heads and crashed into the door—which Dad would then have to fix. But in the back of the car we were sitting ducks and when she unleashed the thing, she really went for it, quite oblivious to the fact (passive smoking aside) that she was leaving herself open to future litigation if she inflicted real damage.

The shoe, a heavy-heeled Homy Ped, tore through the air like a peregrine falcon, the air parting with a high-pitched screaming sound as it did. We leapt about the back like demented frogs as we tried in vain to avoid its swoop. The sound called to mind images of *Batman* as the shoe *BIFFED*, *POWED* and *THWACKED* the vinyl until tragically there emanated from our midst a heavy *THUD*. Trish had curled up into the smallest ball that anatomy and her non-stretch jeans would allow; I leapt onto the window ledge where I was reasonably safe unless Dad suddenly hit the anchors and turned me into a long, thin projectile. But Paul, diving for cover on the floor behind Dad's seat hadn't been so quick and the sudden *THUD* of cork connecting with head was quite alarming—especially if it was your head.

Paul spent the rest of the journey curled up in Mum's arms, and except for the occasional 'There, there', we rounded the endless rim of Lake George in deafening silence.

We paid for it later, though, as Paul opted to cover some of The Dubliners' more raucous compositions. Mum dug into her purse, not to show her appreciation of the music, but because, considering the weight and texture of her shoe, the little trouser-snake was still alive.

Once, before we'd hit Goulburn, Dad remembered a dream he'd had earlier in the week that involved monkeys throwing cows at him and he started snorting. He immediately became incapable of little else for the next hour or so. He was so hysterical by the time we arrived in Goulburn that we had to have a change of driver. This sent a ripple of alarm running along the vinyl. Mum's idea of driving was that all other road users were a complete pack of bastards who were out to get her and *why don't you watch where you're going, idiot!* Apart from Dad's occasional snort, the rest of the trip to Canberra was silent. The thought of Mum reaching for the same shoe that was controlling the accelerator quite literally chilled us to the vinyl.

When we were bored beyond belief we would lie upside-down and play foot-puppets, much to the amusement of the cars behind us. Though, given their speed relative to ours, very brief amusement.

Once, when the Parramatta rugby league team won its grand final, or last game or whatever it was, Paul was trailing his scarf out of Dad's window when the wind from a passing Kenworth dragged it out of his hand. He cried all the way to Mittagong until Mum convinced Dad to turn around and backtrack about ten kays to look for the thing. And when we found it, Dad had to run across four lanes of angry traffic to get it. He gave it to Paul, Mum said, 'There you go, lovey' and hugged him and never once looked like going for her shoe, even though Dad had risked life and limb to retrieve the sodding thing. This showed a distinct lack of consistency in Mum's child-rearing methods. Either Trish or I only had to ask her to wind her window down a fraction so we could breathe and her teeth would start grinding and 'Will you bloody be quiet!'s would join us in the back as a precursor to the landed fish.

All this happened about the time Mum was going through her brief poetry phase and she was actually writing a poem about our mind-numbing road trips, only she couldn't think of a word to rhyme with "Catherine Cookson novel", so Trish suggested she might like to try, "Smoke filled hovel". I thought that was just great. Then I asked her to write a sonnet about how her window didn't seem to go down any further than a finger width, and she cracked the shits and flung the poem out the window. A bit of a shame, because there can't be many poems ten pages long in stream-of-consciousness rhyming couplets about the British Coal Industry in the early sixties, with particular reference to Maltby pit head.

39

Florence Nightingale's Grudge

Despite my permanent pallor and a physique that made me look like a praying mantis on a diet, I was not the unhealthiest child in the world. But like other kids I was prone to coughs, colds, German measles, chicken pox and anything else that happened to be going.

At the first sign of illness Paul, Trish or I would be bundled into Mum and Dad's bed and buried under a pile of blankets and eiderdowns so high that your chest was in danger of collapsing. Dad would be turfed uncomplaining out of his side of the bed and into whichever bed had been vacated by illness.

On one occasion I had caught something quite nasty. I think it was just a common cold that quickly turned into heat exhaustion under all that bedding. Whatever it was, I took a turn for the worse and in my delirious state my mind wandered into the section that stores creativity.

It was early in the evening so Mum and Dad were still up watching *Number 96* while I was sweltering away to nothing in the woollen sauna.

As Abigail's bathrobe cascaded to the floor for about the zillionth time that episode, I woke up screaming that there was a train full of headless ghosts hurtling down our street to collect me because I'd died in my sleep, presumably through dehydration.

At my screams, Mum came bounding into the room and carried me out to the lounge room through the thick fog of their cigarette smoke.

I was lashing out because the ghosts were going to get me and Mum slapped me across the face—not, you understand, because I was interrupting *Number 96*, but because this was how you dealt with anyone who was extremely upset in Maltby. After my sobbing had subsided a bit, I asked if I could go back to bed. I preferred to take my chances with the headless ghosts than the powerful and dangerous hand of my mother.

If I have portrayed Mum as being closer to Mike Tyson than Florence Nightingale, then I need to rectify it immediately. I have never encountered anyone with a better and more caring bedside manner, and, treatment of hysteria aside, there has never been a better nurse. When sickness visited our house you could vomit, piss, shit or literally explode in your bed day or night

John Larkin

and along she would come with a calming smile, soothing flannel, caring word and some industrial-strength cleaning aids. She could change the sheets without your having to leave the bed and quite often without even waking you. During the latter stages of your recuperation, she would be there with toasted soldiers, boiled eggs mashed up in a cup with melted butter, and any number of books, jigsaw puzzles and surprises. And when you were well enough to leave the sick bed she would make you up a special bed on the lounge as a sort of a halfway house. And you would lie there under a Kilimanjaro of blankets, leering at the others because you had the entire lounge to yourself while they had to make do with the single chairs, one of which had a nasty scar in the arm from the time Trish threw a knife at me.

Mum has a heart of gold but the memory of an elephant in hypnotherapy. If you cross her, you cross her for life.

One time Paul had just recovered from the chicken pox. Despite coming under Mum's care he was still feeling a bit fragile when he emerged blinking into the world a fortnight or so later. It was the school holidays so he and Alan Luck wandered down the street to play with Neil Smart, who was the same age. Mrs Smart greeted them at the front door, took one look at Paul, shook her head and said that Alan could come in and play but Paul would have to go home. Poor Paul came running up the street bawling his eyes out, his red hair bobbing in the breeze as he simultaneously wiped his eyes and scratched the remainder of his chicken-pox scabs.

When he told Mum what had happened, she tore out of the house like a whirling dervish on steroids— her progress only slightly impeded by me and Trish being dragged along the ground as we held onto her feet. If Mrs Smart knew how close she came to dying that day she would shudder.

Paul got over the incident almost immediately. He continued to play with Neil and never had a bad word to say about Mrs Smart. But to this day, the mere mention of Mrs Smart's name and Mum will announce that *that woman* should be shot, arrested, drowned, fined, or jailed for being so ugly in a built-up area after 5 pm.

40

The Polecat and the Pencil-case

Whatever it was that Stephen Flannery enjoyed doing, it wasn't having a bath. When you got your first whiff of him your eyes immediately widened to the size of Catherine wheels and the stench just kept coming at you like a pack of dogs at a postman. You had to sit upwind from him if you wanted to stay conscious until the end of the lesson.

My fourth grade teacher, Mr Roberts, was a kind old bloke with an interest in the share market, which he enthusiastically regaled us with daily, despite our glazed expressions. Mr Roberts took one whiff of Stephen Flannery and immediately nicknamed him Polecat. None of us knew what a polecat was, but we assumed it was something that reeked like a dead rat.

Odour aside, Stephen was no oil painting; he was more of an oil stain. But to everyone's amazement, he had a girlfriend. Donna Westward was blonde and quite attractive. If her relationship with Stephen didn't give any indication of her mental state, then her career aspirations did. One rainy lunchtime when we were confined to class, Donna and her best friend Susan Towner turned around and asked me what I wanted to be when I grew up. I told them I intended to be the first kid in space. They giggled and said that they wanted to become strippers. I gulped like someone about to undergo brain surgery without anaesthetic.

'Strippers?' I stammered.

'Yeah,' said Susan. 'We want to take off all our clothes and get paid for it.'

Such was the redirection of blood from my head to my trousers that I almost blacked out. I instantly fantasised them dragging me into the storeroom for a demonstration. In my mind their bottoms had just hit daylight—almost blinding me in the process—when Mr Roberts looked up from his paper and steaming mug and announced that the stock market had fallen. It had a similar effect on me.

Donna and Susan's strippers put my astronaut into some sort of perspective. At least they had set achievable goals. Perhaps Donna had pictured a future with Stephen Flannery that didn't extend further than trailerparks, tv dinners, hairnets and nylon slippers.

Stephen Flannery had already repeated class several times. Mr Roberts warned him constantly that if he didn't knuckle down and do some work, the only job he would be able to get would be sitting on the end of a production line at the Dunlop factory, trimming the excess bits of rubber off tyres. Unfortunately for Mr Roberts, Stephen Flannery saw this as something to aspire to rather than fear. He couldn't believe that someone was willing to pay good money for such a task, and the itinerant future that had been looming before him was instantly replaced with a steady job, a caravan, tv dinners, the TAB guide and a foxy wife who insisted on disrobing at any opportunity.

For all his faults and odours Stephen Flannery did, however, have two things on me: an achievable career goal and a girlfriend who loved to scamper about naked. He was on the lowest rung of the fourth grade ladder but I was jealous of him. It just didn't seem right.

Above the blackboard in our classroom was a speaker about the size of a small cake box. It looked like the sort of thing you might have had at schools in Nazi Germany so that members of Hitler Youth could listen to broadcasts from Der Führer. We listened to songs on ours. The only one I can remember was about a Scottish soldier who was posted overseas, but missed the green hills of home—pined for them right to the end of the song, despite the fact that he was quite clearly dead. I used to feel sad for him and it made me miss Maltby.

At the start of the year, my three best friends, David Griffiths, David Marlin and Neil Ollier, were all in different classes. Indira Narayan and Annette Oakley had left to go to other schools, while Jasmine Robards no longer even looked sideways at me. The days seemed rainy and long so I consoled myself by dipping into a rich fantasy world of strippers, storerooms and the missing hills of Maltby—even though Maltby was as flat as road kill.

In danger of becoming so insignificant that the very particles that held me together seemed eager to disperse and go about their business, I knew I had to do something. The school athletic carnival was my chance to elevate myself in the eyes of my classmates, particularly Jasmine Robards, who was getting more beautiful by the minute.

For some reason both Paul and I could run like the clappers, whatever they were. Mum and Dad, though both keen on sports—particularly Dad, who was a well-known hurler for Tullamore and County Offaly in his day—did not appear to be blessed with speed. By the time I was three and able to store memories, of course, Dad would have been well past his peak. And Mum's ability to run down a departing bus would have been impeded by her handbag, fag, high heels and two toddlers, one of whom kept raining blows on the other. So it's fair to say that I'd really never seen Mum in full flight. And her inability to catch Trish as she tore around the house with a knife or a knitting needle said more for Trish's skill in tight corners than it did about Mum's straight-line speed. No sooner had Mum raised her thigh into a sprint than Trish ducked under the dining room table, through the kitchen and outside to the safety of the bramble patch. The immense forward momentum that Mum generated was absorbed by her Homy Ped shoes, the carpet and the lounge. So Paul and I were never sure where our gift for speed came from. Maybe it was more about survival of the fittest than sporting ability. Just as young Komodo dragons learn to shin up trees to avoid being devoured by their parents, Paul and I had evolved fleetness of foot to escape our sister's scissors, pencil, knife, fork and knitting needle.

Although I couldn't run in third grade due to a virus, by the time I hit fourth I was not only the fastest kid in my year, but the fastest in the entire school.

On the day of the athletic carnival I won all my heats, quarter- and semi-finals easily and lined up in the final, nervous but quietly confident. For some reason Jamie Thorpe, who was in the lane next to me said, 'I'm sorry, but I'm going to beat you now, John.' Jamie was a lovely guy and we later became good friends in high school, but this struck me as an absurd thing to say. Where was the evidence? No one had got near me all day and I'm pretty sure that I could have given the field ten metres start and still run them down. I wasn't being big headed; to me it was a fact, but I shared it with no one. All I had to do was imagine Trish behind me with a kitchen utensil and I could have overtaken a cheetah.

I didn't know where Trish was at that moment, probably behind the hill having a smoke or a snog, rather than destroying the competition in her own race as she clearly could have, but in my mind she was five metres behind me, leering like Boris Karloff.

Almost the whole school had crowded around the track. The tape was stretched tight across the finish line and shimmering in the distance. Without getting into *Chariots of Fire* hype, the gun sounded and my spaghetti legs blurred as I took the lead and won at a canter. I had my fifteen seconds of fame: a few pats on the back and 'Well done!'s, notably from Trish and some of her friends, who hadn't been smoking or snogging at all, but cheering "little bro" on. The hip crowd talked about me for all of thirty seconds and Jasmine Robards couldn't have helped but notice my athletic prowess. But, of course, unless she was mind-meltingly superficial, it was not about to elevate me to snog-worthy.

The fifth and sixth grade finals were run and won, slower than my race but still exciting. But the day had already been stolen by an unlikely thief. As the crowd dispersed into the afternoon, the pats on the back became fewer and fewer until I only had to collect my bag from the hill and walk home. The few kids and teachers who remained, like those who had already gone, were talking about one person: Stephen sodding Polecat Flannery.

Wherever Stephen Flannery went he carried his

pencil-case. I can't imagine what he had in it that had to be carted around twenty-four hours a day. He was not known for his diligence, in fact he was better known for having once turned up for school on a Saturday; not from intellectual hunger, but because he thought it was Friday. I'm still amazed that, as Stephen sauntered past, he never thought to question why Binnalong Oval shrilled with the sounds of weekend soccer, netball and rugby on a Friday.

When I wasn't despising him for stealing my thunder, or laughing at him for doing something stupid, I actually felt quite sorry for him. His family, though hardly rich, could surely have afforded a couple of buttons rather than send him to school with bits of shirt threaded through the buttonholes. It looked bad but it was better than having to look at his birdcage chest. Apart from our sporting, social and intellectual differences, which were not as great as I liked to imagine, we simply moved in different circles. Stephen ran with the sort of crowd who enjoyed sticking a lit bunger up a cat's backside. I didn't. Then I might have mentioned the fact that it was difficult to be anywhere within three metres of him and not want to vomit. This aside, however, there were times that I would look at him and feel compassion. I wished I could take him under my wing— metaphorically, of course—and look after him and help him up the ladder a bit. But in the jungle of the school playground, when you had found your own rung, you tended to reach up rather than down.

Stephen Flannery appeared to accept his lot in life and would have been more than happy to sit on the end of that Dunlop production line, take his pay, go home to his caravan, disrobe with his wife, then mellow out and think his thoughts. He knew where he was going. Okay, it mightn't have been that far, but, unlike the rest of us, he probably got there. Prepared to let life unfold around him, he wasn't governed by drive and ambition, but perhaps by some inner contentment. He might have been the first Buddhist I'd ever met.

His pencil-case was an enigma wrapped in a riddle. The plastic name holder couldn't accommodate "Stephen", "Flannery" or "Polecat" because of all the exclamation marks he insisted on using. So it simply read "Flanno!!!!!!!!!" Whatever it contained, though, will always be a mystery, like the Bermuda Triangle, black holes, electric slippers and the appeal of reality tv. Pencils? Doubtful. Rubbers (the erasing kind)? Maybe, given all the errors he made. But he only saw his mistakes after Mr Roberts had pointed them out and it was too late to correct them. Drugs? Unlikely. Although he acted like he was off his face, this was more likely due to his own powerful odour than any illegal substance in his pencil-case.

Stephen Flannery had arrived at the athletic carnival with his school uniform, packed lunch and his pencil-case. Perhaps he thought it was Saturday again, but then somebody pointed out his mistake. 'Hey Flannery, you idiot. It's the athletic carnival today!'

'Is it?' said Stephen scratching his head and relocating a colony of nits in the process.

'What did you think?' said some wag. 'That we'd all just decided to come and sit on the hill in coloured clothes?'

'I did think it was a bit weird.'

Five hundred children suddenly falling back on the spectators' hill at Binnalong Oval and kicking their thousand legs in the air must have been quite a sight. Unfortunately I didn't get to see it myself, because two of the legs were mine.

The thing about the Toongabbie Primary School athletic carnival was that every student was made to run. You had your age race and if you came first, second or third you got to race again until there were only eight or so left in the final. This was fine if you were sporty or had a psychotic sister to help you train. But if you were one of the fat, wheezy kids who hated games, then it must have been hell. Roland Roundbutt had to be carried to the start of his heats, and although he brandished a note excusing him from the carnival, he was forced to run. So when the gun sounded, he did just that. He turned around and ran up the back hill, into the alley and home. As he did, we could see he was running away from the finishing line faster than the rest of the field were running towards it. He became something of an anti-hero, nerd cult figure for a while—a sort of rebel without a clue—until the position was well and truly taken over by Stephen Flannery.

Stephen eventually took his place on the starting line later that morning. He held onto his rolled up pencil-case as if it was a relay baton. The thing was, he did have some athletic ability. I'd seen him tear across the field playing softball, though admittedly he was running away from a sky ball rather than trying to catch it; and he did go on to swim for the school in year 6. Though, again, this was because he was the only fourteen-year-old in year 6. But on this particular day I figured that his shoes were bound to cause him trouble. At our school athletic carnivals, club sprinters like me were not allowed to wear our spiked shoes. This was reasonable since we had the unfair advantage of being competitive runners to begin with. So everyone ran in bare feet. Everyone except Stephen Flannery, who was told in no uncertain terms by Mr Roberts that if he even thought about removing his shoes, he would be beaten to within an inch of his life. Mr Roberts had decided that the radioactive fallout from Stephen Flannery's shoes might do for Toongabbie what the nuclear power industry eventually did for Chernobyl.

Like most of us, Stephen Flannery owned a pair of Bata school shoes—the ones with the lion paw prints on the soles and the compass in the heel. Unfortunately he'd had them since year 2 and I'm almost certain that he wasn't the original owner. The compass had long since disintegrated and the soles were as smooth as bowling balls.

The starting pistol echoed across the oval and Stephen Flannery took off like the coyote in pursuit of the roadrunner. His legs were just a blur and he would have been quite fast, except for the fact that his frictionless shoes failed to rotate the earth under them. He must have been running on that spot for at least twenty seconds. Eventually physics relented and allowed him some forward momentum, but it was too late and the thousand legs kicking in the air were joined by a thousand fists thumping the ground. The other runners in his race had long finished and now turned around and started to cheer him in. Halfway down the track, his shoelaces, unused to such pressure, broke under the strain and propelled the shoes off his feet and into the air in a high, graceful, steaming arc. Even the two teachers who had retrieved the tape and stretched it across the finishing line again for him collapsed in a heap at the sight of his airborne shoes.

Most of us would have assumed a massive persecution complex if this had happened to us. We would have spent the next ten years sulking and getting heavily into Bob Dylan before applying for a gun licence and a job at the Post Office. Stephen Flannery was made of different stuff. He never actually made it to the finishing line. He collapsed about five metres short, not from exhaustion but from laughter. His pencil-case, its broken zip long ago replaced by a safety pin, had gone the way of his laces and showered its mysterious contents across the track. He was laughing so much at himself that he couldn't walk, let alone run, and had to be helped from the track by a couple of teachers whose eyes were streaming. After about ten minutes, when he had recovered the use of his legs, he made his way slowly to the hill, where he received a standing ovation. He even gave a little bow, which brought a fresh round of applause. And when a teacher handed him the steaming puddles of rubber that had once been his shoes as if they were a bouquet of flowers, fresh howls of laughter clattered across the hill.

The bastard! This was supposed to have been my day, but Stephen Flannery had pinched it from under my nose. If Jasmine Robards had started making moves on him, I would have disappeared in spontaneous combustion.

41

Bowling Outswingers

Home life was good. Mum and Dad worked as much overtime as they could to pay off the mortgage, put in a pool and buy things for the house. This left the three of us with plenty of time on our hands both after school and during the holidays.

Trish was becoming less psychotic but more withdrawn. She'd only caught the end of the hippy age but was still getting into tranquillity, big hair and Buddhism. Her room reeked of incense, henna and herb. She had turned quite artistic, which usually meant that she was still in bed at lunchtime reading John Lennon's *A Spaniard in the Works* or meditating, searching for inner peace and spiritual harmony or yelling at Paul and me to shut the fuck up.

She'd stopped clouting me (I could clout her back by this time) and started arguing with Mum instead. Experience had taught me that you took on a Yorkshire woman at your peril. Mum could fire her slippers at

Trish's bedroom door like a ninja warrior hurled *shuriken*.

Paul, Dad and I kept well clear of the slipper and joss-stick crossfire. Dad would vacuum the pool (we had the cleanest one on the planet) or sit on the back veranda with a beer and think. Paul and I would stage marathon cricket matches in the carport.

The rules for these matches were so complicated that if we'd ever written them all down, the index would have been the size of the *Encyclopaedia Britannica*. For example: a batsman was out if he was bowled, caught (one-handed off the wall or carport frame), adjudged LBW, or if it was his turn to dry the dishes when Mum called. Then there were the obscure laws:

Rule 9. Sub-section C.
A batsman shall be adjudged out if he
breaks the Major's window unless
a: The Lucks aren't in.
b: The Major is at sea.
c: He can dive for cover without being seen.
d: He can blame somebody else.

And the ridiculous:

Rule 137. Sub-section X.
A batsman shall be adjudged out and
forced to make the bowler's bed for a
year and supply him with cups of tea on

demand if he hits the ball over the
back fence and it injures a rooster.

The basic problem in bowling with a tennis ball was
that they just did not swing. Not even slightly. No matter
how long your run-up, how energetic your delivery or
how moist the air, a tennis ball stubbornly refused to
curve. That was, however, before the advent of electrical tape (you taped up half the ball), the carport and
the large block of land next to it, which Dad threat-
ened to—and eventually did—erect a double garage on.
Not that this bothered Paul or me. It took us about
five minutes to incorporate Dad's red brick monolith
into the rules, just as it had taken only thirty seconds
to deal with Trish's frequent and dubious migraines.
"The ball shall be wrapped in a chamois if available or,
failing that, a dry flannel. Should this prove unsuitable,
then several blankets shall be unfurled on the pitch to
absorb the sound of ball striking concrete". I was rather
pleased with this rule especially my use of "unfurled",
even if Paul didn't have a clue what the hell it meant.

But before the garage was built, the carport was the
perfect all-weather cricket pitch. When the rain was hammering like bullets on the roof, the game was interrupted
briefly while the bowler put on his wet-weather gear
and anorak. Once, during a second Noah's flood, Paul
batted for over an hour and amassed a meagre fourteen
runs as the waterlogged ball refused to go anywhere

near the boundary (Lucks' fence) and jarred his hands whenever tape made contact with willow. The *squelch, squelch, squelch* of my run-up was only drowned out by the *swoosh, swoosh, swoosh* of wet-weather gear, which in turn was submerged under the occasional, *'Will you idiots come in this instant?'* as Mum tried to tempt us inside with offers of pies, toasted sandwiches, tea, Tim-Tams, and abuse. The only thing louder was the occasional *'Mum!'* as Trish, buried under her hessian doona with John Lennon, screamed like Yoko Ono every time a top edge found the carport roof. The ball looked like a Catherine wheel as it left the bowler's hand and spun through the air, shedding about a litre of water on its way to the bat.

These day-long matches were only abandoned when Dad arrived home early from work and totally ignored **Rule 42c**: "Under no circumstances will cars be permitted to park in the carport while a match is in progress—except on Thursday night when Mum comes home from grocery shopping and has a tub of Neapolitan ice-cream. The player who has scored the lowest number of runs shall be permitted to eat only vanilla and strawberry."

Meanwhile in the house, the beast slouched towards the tv to be bored.

42

The Message from God

Father Shepherd was an old priest who was nearing the end of his ecclesiastical career—at least in a mortal sense. Father English was, on the other hand, a young upstart with chiselled good looks and thick black hair. No doubt several of his flock had an unconfessable desire to run their hands through it. When you saw him the words "cool" and "dude" sprang instantly to mind. He would practically moonwalk down the aisle and the way he swung his censer suggested that he was wearing very little if anything under that cassock.

Father Shepherd gave the sort of sermons that would put a caffeine-affected canary to sleep: 'And Matthew came upon his tapestry and said unto him, "Tis a fine tapestry that thou hast woven. I particularly like the bold use of yellow to depict the sun and predict that thou shalt receive four score pepper pots for it if thou...".'

Father English's sermons came straight from groove

town. Although Father English held the Catholic line, he certainly gave the boundaries a bit of a nudge. The protagonists in his sermons were more likely to be called Davo and Sharon than Luke and Mary. In short, he was the sort of priest that had young men thinking about the priesthood as a possible career, and some of the women petitioning the Vatican against its draconian rule that priests remain celibate. And what did the Catholic Church do to Father English? Promote him? Summon him to the Vatican to advise the Pope? It got rid of him. That tedious old git, Father Shepherd ascended to the pulpit one Sunday morning and, with a smile playing at the corners of his mouth, announced that Father English had gone on leave.

They certainly gave him some holiday, because as far as I know he's still on it. I always imagined that he had run off to Hawaii with one of the more voluble members of the church choir. But everyone knew that Father Shepherd was lying through his teeth, and that the very eccentricity that had wooed so many to the church had proven too much for the conservative corpses who ran it. So Father English was shipped off to Fartsville NSW, where there were three parishioners and a sheep.

It was back to Father Shepherd's eye-glazing sermons, which were livened up just once when an extremely agitated man stormed the altar. When he started taking off his clothes, everyone realised that this wasn't a piece of impromptu street theatre directed by

the exiled Father English. After the shock and mur-
muring had died down, the man started gyrating his
hips and pointing at an imaginary mirror ball somewhere overhead. His performance climaxed with an
announcement that he had a message from God. Before
he could reveal what it was, however, six of the burli-
est members of the congregation jack-booted their way
up to the altar and dragged the poor guy off. They
carted him down the aisle in the most undignified
manner—his head down and his arms and legs splayed
out to the side. I seemed to be the only one even vaguely
aware of the irony. The only thing missing was his crown
of thorns.

I've often wondered what happened to the poor soul
outside. Maybe Father Shepherd's henchmen thought
he was possessed by the devil and proceeded to beat
nineteen types of shite out of him. Maybe they sat him
down with a cup of tea and talked over his issues.
Perhaps, free of their clutches, he tore across the road
to the newsagent and announced that he had a message
from Rupert Murdoch. And, having done that, came
bounding back across the road to Jack Crumbly's Bike
and Lawn-mower Exchange with a message of a more
mechanical nature. The thing was that if the guy claimed
to have a message from God—and in Toongabbie he
was as good a source as any—then I for one would have
liked to hear it.

Father English would have woven the incident into

his sermon, or given the guy a high-five and then arranged to meet him afterwards for a coffee and a chat. He would have preached to the congregation a week later about the need for greater understanding of mental illness and those less fortunate. But the poor bloke was turfed out of church like a drunk from a pub so that Father Shepherd could get back to his sermon. 'And Andrew came to Peter and said unto him, "Hast thou devoured my donut?" and, seeing that he had been sprung, Peter said, "Verily, I stuffed it in my gob and it surpassed all other donuts." And Andrew saw the hundreds and thousands on the ground and knew that he spake the truth. And there was wailing and gnashing of teeth.'

Something like that; I'd gone back to sleep.

After what happened to God's messenger I lost all interest in organised religion and became immensely wary of so-called authority figures. I still went to church on Sunday; it was the only thing Dad ever asked me to do, so I was happy to tag along. But not long after, I heard the echo of the car out in the cricket pitch one Sunday morning and realised that Dad had gone without me. And while I gained an extra hour or so in bed, when he stopped asking me to go with him, I lost something too.

43

Helen of Toongabbie

By the start of year 6 I had fallen in love again. I was still in love with Jasmine Robards and would continue to be for rest of my school days. Not that she would ever know. It was a difficult subject to broach after four years. After eight it just seemed absurd. So I had to let her go, chalk that one down to experience and move on.

If Helen of Troy's face had launched a thousand ships, then Helen Edmundson's could have turned them around and smashed them into kindling.

Unlike Jasmine Robards, Annette Oakley and Indira Narayan, however, Helen Edmundson was a girl I could actually engage in conversation without wanting to give her ponytail a good, solid yank and then run off and hide.

At the start of year 6 our teacher, Ray Fearn, sat me next to her. It was a move I can only put down to great karma. I never missed a day for the entire year and my grades went through the roof.

Ray Fearn was a huge and charismatic New Zealander. While he taught the syllabus he added in many life lessons as well. And he was fun. He took us out to the soccer fields behind the school and let us scream the haka at the top of our lungs. It was great. He was so popular that when Heather Foster accidentally smashed his guitar, we ran a collection to buy him a new one. Okay we might have scraped together only $2.48 (barely enough to buy him a string and a pick) but it was a thought. The only trouble with having a brilliant teacher like Ray was that it spoiled you for all teachers who came after him. You only got one and my subsequent years in the wilderness at Pendle Hill High, I eventually realised, were due to there being no Ray Fearns on the staff.

When I noticed that Helen Edmundson covered her books with horse posters, I immediately shelved my plans for becoming a soccer-playing astronaut and decided on a career as a roustabout instead. Although she and I never actually *went* with each other, this was mostly because we were too young to go anywhere. Even if there'd been somewhere to go to, I probably wouldn't have been allowed to take her. Most of the kids in our class assumed we were going together, though.

I had friends who were going with girls. My best friend in year 6, Mark Savage, was going with several girls at once. But he could get away with it because he was drop-dead handsome and wore Hawaiian shirts to school. He was quite mature for his age and seemed more interested in going with one of the teachers than any of the girls he was actually going with. The teacher concerned, however, was going with her husband, who was also a teacher at the school. For a whole year I didn't go with any other girls, just in case Helen decided that she wanted to go with me after all. I wanted to be available.

Everyone knew that I went to the farewell dance with Corina Matteo, because Helen couldn't come with me or had decided to go with someone else. That is, I didn't actually *take* Corina to the dance, dance with her, or even set eyes on her the whole evening—she may even have stayed at home sick. But I did go with her and that was the main thing. Instead, Neil Ollier and I ducked out the back with Mark Savage and took turns at chugging some concoction Mark had thrown together from his father's bar. After my third swig, Mark's new Hawaiian shirt looked like it was battery operated. By the seventh, I was crying on his shoulder because I would never get to go with Helen Edmundson.

Helen hated Mark's smugness, although this hadn't stopped her from going with him a couple of times during the year.

On the last day of primary school I gave her a hug and I said that I would see her the following year at Pendle Hill High. Helen said that she was sorry but she was going to a different school—Northmead. Then she smiled, turned round and walked out of my life and into my books forever.

Six weeks later, when high school started, I'd given up girls as a bad joke. Instead I spent most of my teenage years going with myself.

44

Sid Vicious's Cat

Every afternoon when school was out, Darryl Nelson, Michael Luck, Tony O'Neil, the new kid in our street, Randell Easthorpe, and I played soccer. Tony and I both had a set of portable quarter-size goal posts, which we would carry over to the Marist Fathers' to begin our marathon games. We played until it was too dark to see the ball. It didn't matter if it was bucketing down, if a gale had blown up from the south, or the mercury had hit forty. After several years of this we all became accomplished players and saw soccer as a definite career possibility. Randell and I eventually went on to play in the Australian National League—Randell even managed to sit on the bench for Australia and had trials with Liverpool in England. Darryl played briefly in the State League and Millwall's youth team. Tony and I spent three months training with Derby County (his parents' home town) as seventeen-year-olds, and were as good as, if not better, than any of the other seventeen-year-olds there at the time. Neither of us, though, could handle the thought of living in Derby, so we returned home to the Marist Fathers'. It was a pretty impressive output for one street. From the five of us, only Michael realised that professional soccer playing wasn't a career option. So he joined the public service and moved to Canberra.

But I'm getting ahead.

I started high school and started writing. Not for anyone but myself. I wrote poems mostly, but short stories and philosophy also got a look in. My subject was the usual teen angst about girls, pimples, and the way Mum had made me turn up for high school that first day with my pants up around my chest and how I'd earned the nickname Spaghetti Legs as a result.

Jasmine Robards was in my class, but she didn't seem even remotely aware of my existence. Nor did any of the other girls.

Not wanting to stand out from the crowd academically, I retreated to the back row and played the class clown. The maths teaching that drifted towards us must have been absorbed or diluted along the way, because there was practically nothing left by the time it finally reached the back row. I gazed at algebra equations until my eyes bled. I was suffering some sort of mathematical dyslexia. So I spent the best part of my first two years at Pendle Hill High singing Queen's *Bohemian*

Rhapsody with Neil Ollier and Dean Bracey and staring at the poster of the old woman next to an empty bird-cage with a caption that read, "Polygon" and thinking it was absolutely brilliant.

At night I would sit up in bed reading, or writing Monty Pythonish sketches that our wonderful English teacher, Miss Simpson, let me perform in class. My favourite was the one where Sid Vicious tries to feed his cat. Sid arrives home from a hard night's gobbing on people at a Sex Pistols concert, but his house is in such chaos that he can't find his can opener. He tears around the house effing and blinding, making more mess and threatening to bring down the government if it doesn't return his can opener this $%#&%$# instant. My classmates loved it, but I felt the subtleties of the skit might have gone over their heads. They were laughing at my effing and blinding, but of course the real joke was Sid Vicious having a cat.

Encouraged by Miss Simpson, I carried on writing. I wrote about school and what I thought of it. I wrote about soccer and what I thought of that. I wrote about *Monty Python's Flying Circus* and what I thought of *that*. I wrote about summer holidays and the sudden arrival of the Mr Whippy van in our street and how you had to run across the bindii patches and red hot asphalt in bare feet like a Polynesian firewalker to get to it, and what I thought of that. I wrote about Helen Edmundson going to a different high school and *exactly* what I thought of that.

As much as I loved writing, though, I didn't see it as a career, or even a back-up. My left foot was a gift from God. I wouldn't need a back-up career. I briefly considered becoming a doctor, but I was so anaemic looking it would have been bad for business. You couldn't look sicker than your patients.

But a writer, coming from my background? Forget it! Writers didn't grow up in Maltby and Toongabbie with brief interludes on board the *Achille Lauro* and in Georges Hall. No. They lived in lighthouses, windmills, castles, or mansions with a well out the back. And when *they* were young they lived in the countryside and wore shorts down to their knees and shirts with collars and sleeveless pullovers. During the summer holidays they put hamsters in boxes and raced them down stream. After lunch they went for long bike rides even further into the countryside and watched undetected while Farmer Thrasher's daughter skinny-dipped in the river. Then they generally needed to duck behind a tree for about ten seconds. They had a best friend called Tristram Bannister-Smythe who was an aviation buff, owned the complete back-set of *Biggles* novels and maintained a peculiar interest in badgers. Together they restored an old World War II Spitfire in a refurbished barn with regular breaks to cycle out into the countryside to watch

Farmer Thrasher's daughter. They, in short, had interesting lives. Lives worth writing about.

You couldn't have my background and become a writer. It didn't work like that. Most of the Monty Python boys had gone to Cambridge and had performed in the famous "Footlights", and probably still kept up their peculiar interest in badgers.

What would *I* ever write about? *My* friends? No one would be interested in reading about *my* friends. What, for instance, did John Averyham ever do that was worth writing about?

45

The Red Rattler and the Bandsaw

John Averyham had the greasiest hair I had ever seen. He didn't so much comb it as change the oil every two thousand kays. This was pre-mousse and hair-gel so John must have been pasting down his thatch with industrial quantities of Brylcreem. The rest of us got up in the morning and tried to tame our hair with wet hands and damp combs. This lasted until we were about halfway to school, where it immediately leapt back up and spent the rest of the day there. John, however, always turned up at school looking immaculate, from the shine of his shoes, the crisply ironed crease in his regulation long trousers, to the lint-free socks with ribbing that ran in complete mathematical harmony with the local ley lines. His shirt was so sharp and fresh it still had pins in it, while his hair was only marginally less shiny than his shoes. It looked as if he had borrowed his entire head from the first Darren Stevens in *Bewitched* while the rest of us had to make do with looking more like Endora. We did wonder about the long-term effect of having that much inflammable oil up on top. Ian Drinan and Paul Campion, the brains of our group, once tried to estimate how much had seeped into his skull. It certainly went some way to explaining some of the odd things John Averyham did.

Most of the guys in the group—Gary Wright, Neil Ollier, Glenn Davis, Jamie Thorpe, Glen Kelly, Philip Fernie, Greg Birtles, Adam Young, Shane Pritchard and Dean Bracey—were naturally good at one sport or another, but if they applied themselves were also capable of getting good grades in class. Ian Drinan and Paul Campion were naturally brainy, but if they applied themselves they were capable of being good at sport. Nature seemed to compensate for your ordinariness in one area with success in another. But John Averyham had missed out all round. He carted round a Stanley Stamford school case, and that, along with his immaculate clothes, made him look intellectual, but the appearance was deceptive. If you whispered a question to him during a test, he looked thoughtful for a moment then lapsed into a long but coherent explanation that he didn't have the foggiest clue what the answer was.

He was so uncoordinated when it came to sport that I used to think he was doing it for a joke. When you saw him with a cricket stick, a baseball racquet or tennis club, he was so hopeless that you could only conclude he was trying to invent an entirely new game. Or that he was in the middle of a complicated semaphore transmission to someone in the Blue Mountains. During a softball game he could use up his own three strikes as well as several of his team-mates' at just one pitch. It was like watching a helicopter prepare for take-off.

He was once given six of the best for taking out Jamie Thorpe with a hockey stick. Unable to get near the ball, he launched his stick at Jamie's head in frustration. Jamie had gone tearing up the wing with the ball, when suddenly John's hockey stick went *THWOCKA THWOCKA THWOCKING* over our heads like an enormous boomerang. For the first time in his life, John had scored a perfect hit. He was marched off to the headmaster's office with his head held high.

Another time I watched him take a swipe at a soccer ball and miss it so spectacularly that the enormous follow-through sent his horizontal body into orbit. His buttocks had obviously been hardened by a lifetime of similar mishaps and when he plummeted back to earth, the impact produced merely a resigned sigh. It would have killed anyone else.

John's family belonged to some religious organisation that would banish him to hell for even looking at a can of Coke or a chocolate bar, but was quite comfortable with his leaping from trains.

Midway through year 8 we were all taken on an

excursion to the Sydney Museum to see the Neanderthal exhibition. The visit gave some kids in the top stream an opportunity to consider a career in archaeology or anthropology; it gave some of the others a chance to study the more recent branches on their family trees.

On the train ride back from town, the teachers abandoned any attempts at control and let anarchy reign. The doors on the old red rattlers weren't automatic, and for most passengers they were too cumbersome to close. So at one point I poked my head out the carriage door, looked back and saw about forty other heads sticking out of various openings. The glare coming from the back of the train was obviously from Mark Savage's latest Hawaiian shirt. We were like dogs in a Kombi van. How we avoided losing our heads altogether I do not know.

Anyway, this day the train was just coming into Pendle Hill station when John Averyham, in the interest of scientific enquiry and perhaps to alleviate the boredom, decided to see if he could half-alight and scooter one foot along the platform. Unfortunately for John his coordination wasn't good and in attempting to only half-alight and skip his trailing leg, he fully alighted and ended up running alongside the train at a speed that was simply beyond him. Cheered on by the whole of year 8, John was propelled along the platform like a demented gazelle as he tried to stay upright and out of hospital—neither of which he managed. No one knew for sure what speed the train was doing that day, but the sparks that flew from John Averyham's Stanley Stamford as it thundered along beside him suggested that it must have been pretty fast. At one point John actually began to overtake the train, presumably because even the old red rattlers had a more sophisticated braking mechanism than the school shoes of a fourteen-year-old boy.

When John was finally released from the trauma ward at Westmead Hospital and had returned to school, he'd hardly had time to pause for breath when, out of sheer curiosity, he decided to see if the non-cutting side of the bandsaw blade could be put to some purpose—such as removing the crusts from his sandwiches or sawing a block of wood in half. Neil Ollier, Gary Wright, Shane Pritchard, Jamie Thorpe and I watched in wonder as the blunt side of the bandsaw quickly took care of John's sandwich crusts before starting in on the block of wood. It would probably have cut the block in half too, if it hadn't suddenly encountered a nine-inch nail and John's middle finger, both of which managed to impede its progress in varying degrees.

Mr Lemur our dwarfish woodwork/French teacher (not an obvious combination) bounded up to us speaking in tongues. It was interesting to learn that 'Just what the fuck is going on here?' sounds roughly the same, no matter which language it's spoken in. But we'd never been able to respect anyone who looked like a frog and was fond of eating their hind legs too. We fell about laughing. Meanwhile John galloped about trying to stem the flow of blood with a handkerchief that he kept in his top pocket for just that purpose. Mr Lemur stood there moaning about the destruction of his Anglo-French bandsaw in what sounded like Latin.

46

Crime and Punishment

During a language lesson given by the wonderful Ms McDonald I found myself turfed out of class. I'd deliberately mispronounced an Indonesian word so that it sounded vaguely rude and Ms McDonald, who was normally a bit of a pushover, sent me outside. I stood there contemplating my crime, wondering whether Jasmine Robards had laughed at my brilliant wit and doubting it. While I was waiting for Ms McDonald to let me back in, I noticed several other boys standing outside *their* classrooms. Presumably they were guilty of linguistic, historical or scientific crimes too, since E-Block was mostly reserved for these subjects.

My thoughts were interrupted by the *whoosh* of bamboo slicing through the air, followed by a loud *thwack*.

Mr Whitmont, a bit of a linguistic criminal himself, had obviously enjoyed the experience and gazed over the balcony to see the seven or eight of us below.

He must have almost had an accident in his embarrassingly high walk-shorts. He strutted down the stairs like John Wayne in white knee-high socks and zip-up canvas shoes and proceeded to cane each of us in turn, including the unfortunate year 7 kid who had just popped out to go to the toilet. 'YOU SHOULD HAVE GONE BEFORE YOU WENT TO CLASS!'

Swoosh.

Swoosh.

Swoosh. THWACK.

'And what have you done, Pat Larkin's brother?' Trish, or Pat as she was now known, was turning just like the ugly duckling into an attractive young woman (or swan, to stick with the metaphor). And she was very popular at school. Like many people, including me, Mr Whitmont found it hard to believe that Trish and I emerged from the same gene pool.

'Well?' he snapped. 'I said what have you *done,* Pat Larkin's brother?'

'I mispronounced a word, sir.'

Swoosh.

Swoosh. THWACK.

'Stupid old prick.'

'WHAT DID YOU SAY?'

'I said that hurt a bit.'

'Good. Hold out the other hand.'

'But, sir, I'm left-handed.'

'So's the devil.'

SWOOSH.

SWOOSH.

SWOOSH.

'Hold still!'

'I am. You keep missing.'

SWOOSH.

SWOOSH.

SWOOSH.

SWOOSH.

'How about you bring the cane down and I'll move my hand under it?'

'You're trying my patience, Pat Larkin's brother.'

SWOOSH.

SWOOSH.

SWOOSH.

'Today would be good.'

'Quiet! Pat Larkin's brother.'

SWOOSH.

SWOOSH. CRUNCH.

'Ouch! You got my wrist, you...'

'Now get back inside and let that be a lesson to you.'

'You stupid old turd.'

But he'd moved on. 'That boy there. You, cleaning the duster. Come here!'

I went back into class to the expected round of sniggers.

As I sat down Ms McDonald said, 'I'm sorry, John. You didn't deserve that.'

'That's okay, Miss, it wasn't your fault. He's an idiot.' Ms McDonald let my comment pass, possibly because she felt she owed me one because the punishment did not fit the crime, but I think because she agreed with me.

Mr Whitmont wasn't a bad man; in fact he was one of the more likeable teachers at the school. But he was one of many who had lost the plot and were merely going through the motions of teaching. He'd been my Latin and French teacher on and off for two years and all he'd ever given me before was the nickname "Spider Writer" because I wrote with my left hand and smudged my writing. But I'd had Ray Fearn for just one year and he'd given me many of the building blocks for life.

47

Happy Birthday

My fifteenth birthday arrived with cards, presents, good wishes, intense pain and eventual hospitalisation.

Australian schoolboys have a tradition of giving the birthday boy a punch on the arm for every year of his age. This is usually done surrounded by close friends and, as Freud would have seen at once, is the male equivalent of a girly hug. At Pendle Hill High, though, we had no time for Freud, and birthdays existed not for celebrating your good fortune at having been born, but for wishing that you hadn't.

I thought I'd managed to keep my birthday quiet. But in first period history, Ms Nej announced with a scowl that this was Adolf Hitler's birthday, a memory was obviously triggered somewhere deep in Neil Ollier and Gary Wright. They both began to leer at me like voyeurs at a peep show.

On the way to our next class they swaggered up to wish me many happy returns.

'Not so loud!' I pleaded. 'Kelly might hear you.'
Glen Kelly punched harder than anyone in our year, and
despite being one of the group, I didn't want to be on
the end of one of *his* punches, jokey or otherwise.

'HAPPY B...' Gary began and I quickly covered his
mouth.

The two of them taunted me all morning. At recess
we regrouped and agreed that it would be better for
everyone if I went to the canteen and got their morning
teas—a task they normally reserved for Jamie Thorpe or
John Averyham, both of whom were always after Neil's
approval. Later I went and bought their lunches, but
the whole thing was too much for them to sit on. I'd
just started tucking into my Chiko Roll when they
wished me a loud and succinct happy birthday.

My eyes were the size of frisbees. Though maths
wasn't my best subject, I quickly calculated the number
of punches I was in for: X (age of recipient) × 2 (number
of arms per puncher) × Y (number of boys @ school).
It was the most inspired equation ever to come out of
Pendle Hill High and with five hundred boys on the
roll (and on *a* roll) I was looking at close to 1985
punches. There was a one-armed kid in year 11. I should
point out that, despite the number, the punches themselves weren't necessarily painful. Pendle Hill students
didn't set out to maim anyone. Rarely was the birthday
boy fatally injured; just inconvenienced by being on the
bottom of a five-hundred-strong scrum.

When Neil and Gary announced that it was my birthday I leapt to my feet like a startled meerkat. From my boxed-in position between the canteen and B-Block, my plan was to race up the small incline to the basketball courts, turn right and tear down the hill to the bottom oval which was out of bounds at lunchtime, fly past the animal enclosure, down the alley onto Bulli Road, and then home.

Unfortunately, though, my friends knew that if I accelerated to top speed they'd never be able to catch me and give me the beating I so desperately needed. I had just hit the perfect sprint—high knee-lift, good cadence and long fast strides—when Glenn Davis, no slouch over the hundred himself, grabbed my jumper and hung on for all he was worth. He was stronger than me. The school cat was stronger than me. Glenn just held his ground and left me running on the spot like Stephen Flannery in his year 4 heat. My friends set about me in a jokey, good-natured, half-arsed manner. But it was the arriving hordes, summoned by Jamie Thorpe's loud war cry, that set my pulse racing. I was buried by a torrent of legs and arms, like Pompeii under Vesuvius.

My arms were still numb as I rode my bike to soccer training that afternoon.

I met up with a few of the team outside the milk bar near the railway station and we had our usual four potato scallops and chocolate milkshake before we pedalled our way down Toongabbie's main street to Girraween Park.

It was as I was tying my boots in the change-room that I realised I was in for another pounding. Some of the team went to my school. Three of them, Gary Wright, Glenn Davis and Glen Kelly were in the group. I stood up and started nervously to the door, hoping that no one would notice. But Glenn Davis, who was already responsible for most of my pain that day, looked at me and smiled. 'Happy birthday, John!'

Anyone walking past Girraween Park on 20 April, 1978 would have witnessed a bizarre spectacle. There was a rather thin boy being pursued by three entire soccer teams, including the reserves and some of their friends who didn't actually play but turned up to training for reasons best known to themselves. He hurdled the cyclone fence around the oval with superb technique, took a flying leap at the two-metre-high back fence and slithered down again because he was wearing soccer boots. He took a couple of steps back and launched himself at the fence once more, scurried up it and suddenly stopped when someone grabbed hold of his feet as he reached the top. Then he fell headfirst to the ground, groaned when he brought his right knee down to break the fall and despite his injuries bounced like a dead cat under a speeding tyre.

Anyone walking past that day would have seen this kid tear off down Toongabbie's main street like a greyhound with haemorrhoids. And that person would have been a complete bastard not to stop and offer assistance. Yes, I remember you: the bald guy with the stupid-looking dog and the big shot businessman in the expensive suit and overcoat, with leather gloves and briefcase. If you were the big shot your kit suggested, what were you doing living in Girraween?

I sought sanctuary in the church. No one was going to rumble me there, unless I tried to pass on a message from God. And there was no way my team-mates would follow me onto consecrated ground. With the noise of their boots on the marble floor they'd attract the wrath of Father Shepherd, which some of them had done before.

I made the sign of the cross and hobbled down the aisle. My boot studs clattered over the floor and echoed off the walls. I made another sign of the cross and slid into the second pew. I wasn't there to pray. For a start I couldn't kneel and no amount of worshipping was going to knit my knee back together. And besides, I was flirting with atheism so I felt hypocritical being there at all, even though I was now a fully qualified Catholic. I dabbed tentatively at the source of greatest pain. My kneecap had practically shattered on impact, but now that I had stopped running it blew up like an angry puffer fish. It was sheer agony, far worse than I would have expected from a broken bone. And then I saw what looked like a tiny thorn sticking in my knee. As I hit the ground I had obviously landed on a bee and it had stung me. (I swear I'm not making this up.)

I sat there for ages biting the back of the pew in front to stop myself from screaming with the pain. When the throb of the bee sting had finally subsided a bit, I figured it was safe to venture outside again.

I didn't have any money for the phone, and I wasn't going to ask Father Shepherd. So I had no choice but to leave my bike back at the change-rooms and hobble home. It was the longest, slowest home stretch of my life.

Gary Wright phoned in the evening to say that he had taken my bike home with him and the next day Mum took me to see Dr Singh, who said I had a shattered patella and pharyngitis.

Dr Singh was a lovely man but the practice of medicine was clearly not his strong point. You could go to him with a severed limb, a collapsed lung, or a loose head and he would write you out a prescription and medical certificate for pharyngitis. I can appreciate that English was not his first language, though he spoke it well enough. But, I suppose, having mastered the fiendishly difficult spelling of such a word as "pharyngitis", he intended to use it wherever he could.

Unable to treat anything other than pharyngitis, Dr Singh referred me to an orthopaedic surgeon who amazingly agreed with the first part of his diagnosis.

I was operated on two weeks later. The butcher of a surgeon removed about a third of my kneecap and, looking at my knee even now, I'm convinced that he made his initial incision by taking a thirty-metre run-up with a set of hedge-trimmers.

I started the long recovery process and was off school for about three months. I politely refused Michael Luck's kind offer to bring work home for me. What a swat! As if I was going to waste twelve weeks rest and recuperation doing trigonometry equations and wondering why the German language had three types of "the" and exactly where to use them. Who gave a monkey's? I was going to be a professional soccer player, probably the greatest the world has ever seen, and education was for those losers who only dreamt of doing the things with a soccer ball that I could do. The fact that I'd just damaged my knee beyond repair was irrelevant. Of course, if I'd been a horse I would have been shot.

I went back to school thinner and even more reserved than before.

Everyone else seemed to have moved on with their lives, while I had hobbled on the spot. I'd missed three months of schooling and knew I had no chance now of catching up; or rather, I was too lazy to be bothered. I was going to bide my time, do as little study as possible, stare out the window and dream of future soccer glory.

Or that was the plan.

48

The Psychotic Professor

As they called the roll on my first day back, Jamie Thorpe told me in a voice quivering with panic, that our science teacher—the excellent Mr Slack—had left and now we had Mr Napalm (not his real name).

I gulped.

Mr Napalm was a raving psychopath. He was someone who should never have been allowed to teach children. He was, or so the rumour went, an American Vietnam veteran. If this was true then it's possible that he never fully returned from his tour of duty and in his mind he was still stalking through the jungles of Vietnam. I'd never actually seen Mr Napalm dive under his desk when the Channel 7 News helicopter hurtled by, though it wouldn't have surprised me if he did.

When second period science arrived I took a seat on the third bench. I figured that I would be out of reach (Mr Napalm had a reputation for literally hauling kids out of class) and yet distant enough from the back row, where the tough kids sat and trouble lurked.

After a couple of minutes deafening silence, Mr Napalm turned and scowled at the class—his top lip curled and trembled like a weasel's. He wasn't our roll call teacher, but he insisted on taking his own roll.

As he started with the "Abbots", "Andersons" and "Bowers", I heard Jamie Thorpe whispering my name through clenched teeth from the bench behind. He was risking dismemberment by trying to attract my attention. But there was no way I was turning around.

'Hollows?'

'Here, sir.'

'Kirkwood? Just let me catch whoever that is *WHISPERING* and you'll see exactly what hap*PENS*.'

I could hear Jamie's sphincter tightening.

'Kirkwood?'

'Here, sir.'

'Larkin?'

'Here, sir.'

He looked up from the roll.

'Larkin?'

'Here, sir.' Obviously my return after such a long absence had thrown him out.

'John Larkin.'

'Yes, sir?'

He looked at me as if I was a maggot.

'*John LarKIN!*'

My own sphincter clenched. I had obviously broken some sort of law governing the consumption of oxygen. I couldn't think what else I'd done, sitting there like a petrified stick. 'Yes.'

'*OUT.*' *Quiver. Snarl. Dribble.* '*SIDE.*'

I could feel every single eye trained on me as I got up and limped slowly out of class.

I stood outside trembling and wondering what on earth I had done.

The door closed and Mr Napalm stood opposite me. His cold shark-eyes glared through me and I thought *bollocks to atheism.* I prayed silently that if the Creator would help me through this, I'd go to church every Sunday, regardless of Father Shepherd's eye-glazing ser-mons. But God was tied up elsewhere making statues cry or whatever, and once again I was on my own.

'What. Do. You. Think. You. Are. Up. *TO?*' His voice was steady, yet full of menace, like a picketing docker running an iron bar along a metal fence. Because I wasn't up to anything and my vocal cords had seized up, I said nothing.

'*WELL!*'

'I don't know what you mean.'

'What do you mean, you don't know what I *MEAN?*'

'I just—'

He cut me off with a dangerous sneer. A menacing pause hung in the air between us. Saliva lurked at the corners of his mouth.

'When I allocate you a seat you *STAY IN IT*!' As his inflection changed, he struck out with a hand that stopped just short of my face. Or that must have been his intention, based on long practice in both his teaching and military careers. But he hadn't counted on the advanced state of my nose, which was longer and pointier than the average teenager's. My reaction at being touched was to jolt backwards. I hit my head against the wall and my bladder desperately tried to void itself all over his shoes. This is a defence mechanism passed down to schoolboys by primitive man who, at the first sign of danger, urinated all over his sabre-tooth tiger loin-cloth so that a T-Rex or hungry friend wouldn't be tempted to eat him.

Of course it wasn't Mr Napalm's fault for hitting me but mine for having a longer than average nose that had thrown out his normally impeccable timing.

Apparently I had sat in the wrong spot. That's all. Unlike the other teachers at Pendle Hill, Mr Napalm was so anally retentive he was in constant danger of sucking up his own stool. The only reason he went to the bother of calling his own roll every morning was to make sure that we were all where we should have been. Unfortunately he wasn't where *he* should have been—heavily sedated, with his arms tied securely behind his back.

I saw nothing wrong with Mr Napalm's seating arrangements and would happily have complied with them, if only he'd bothered to tell me about them in the first place. As I walked back into class with a tingling nose, head and bladder, I still didn't know where I was supposed to sit. Fortunately Jamie Thorpe pointed at the spare stool next to him. I grabbed my bag, sat down in the right place and tried to make myself even thinner and more irrelevant than before.

Jamie had stuck his neck out for me, but I had just ten words for him when we were finally free of Mr Napalm's facial contortions at the end of the longest period I'd ever endured: *'Why the hell didn't you tell me at roll call?'*

But Mr Napalm wasn't with us for long. A new permanent teacher joined the staff and Mr Napalm was free to go about whatever it was he did when he wasn't literally scaring the piss out of kids—planning a raid on the Vietnamese restaurant in Parramatta, I imagine.

If Mr Napalm taught me one thing, though, it was that fear and learning are mutually exclusive. I couldn't successfully complete an alkaline test or light a Bunsen burner without setting fire to half the lab when we had Mr Slack, and he was a really nice man. But I knew I'd get there eventually. I couldn't do it in Mr Napalm's class either, but now I was scared shitless because I couldn't.

I heard a few years later that Mr Napalm had been caught in the back of his car with a year 12 girl at the school dance. Another rumour had it that he'd eventually gone too far and had dangled a kid over a first floor balcony by his ankles; probably for having his socks pulled up unevenly. My brother Paul's wife, Linda, who also went to the same school, recently told me that she remembered Mr Napalm entering a class and a girl simply wet herself.

If we could see that Mr Napalm needed help, why couldn't his fellow teachers or the principal, Mr Kemp? Surely they can't have been so concerned with their choice of body-shirt and flares every morning that they had failed to notice a psychopath on the loose.

Thanks to Ray Fearn, I'd entered Pendle Hill High School studious and intelligent, with hopes of going to university and perhaps becoming a doctor or a writer. But now because of teachers like Mr Napalm, I was allowed to slip through the cracks and spiral out of control without doing a scrap of work the whole time I was there and without anyone noticing or caring.

I was part way through year 9 and ready to walk out and get a job in a factory until my soccer career took off. But then I fell in love again and decided to stick around for a bit longer.

49

There's a Mermaid in My German Class

Leanne Doulton had hair of shimmering gold and the face of a Botticelli angel. She sat across the aisle from me in German and I was besotted. When she flicked the hair out of her eyes I had to bite my knuckle to stop myself from screaming. I didn't care if the capital of West Germany was not Berlin or Munich, but Bonn. Nor did I give a monkey's that a *Kugelschreiber* was a pen. I was so totally in love with Leanne Doulton that if Mr Napalm had punched me I would have chimed.

Short of setting fire to myself, though, there seemed to be nothing I could do to get Leanne to notice me. My hilarious one-liners lost something in the translation.

Then one day as I was gazing at Leanne's profile and quietly going insane, I noticed that the fan directly above her was wobbling precariously. If it fell, I would leap across the room, like Spiderman, and save her life. The blades would strike me a vicious blow across one eye. I would be a hero, just like Peter Brady was when he saved that little girl from the collapsing toyshop wall in episode 2265 of *The Brady Bunch*. Leanne would fall passionately in love with me and would never dump me because every time she looked me in the eye, the horrible scar and sightless ball staring back would remind her of my sacrifice. But no matter how hard I gazed at the wobbling fan it flatly refused to fall.

Then it occurred to me that if I could unscrew the nuts I might help it along and speed my way into Leanne's heart, the way that Brooke Shields' boyfriend did in *Endless Love* when he torched her house. Of course he totally overestimated his fire-fighting ability—and the resulting inferno landed him in jail for a very long time.

I didn't want to set Leanne's house on fire. For a start, I wasn't sure how well fibro burned. I had also heard that it contained dangerous levels of asbestos, so that ruled out arson. Unless, of course, I could get hold of some scuba gear to guide Leanne and her family through the roaring blaze to safety. Though my turning up in scuba gear so far from the ocean might raise a few suspicions, so it was back to my original plan to drop rapidly propelling blades on her head. But being totally useless at just about everything, I realised that I would first need an engineering degree and then major facial reconstruction surgery if I was successful. So all that was left was to ponder and pine.

Leanne's shimmering hair was not the gift of some old gypsy woman, who had blessed her at birth with hair of finest silk, but cursed her to sit under wobbling electrical appliances. She belonged to a swimming club. I knew because there were other kids at school—all competitive swimmers—with the same colour hair.

It was obvious what I had to do to get Leanne's attention. What an idiot I'd been! I abandoned all thoughts of fans and facial surgery and started washing my hair in pool chlorine. Leanne would know that I was a swimmer too and therefore relatively snog-worthy. I wasn't stupid, though. I knew that chlorine could burn. So I diluted it: 1 part chlorine. 25 parts water. 2 parts Green Apple shampoo. The preparation I put into this was considerable. I had reached a sort of Zen level of obsession. If I'd put one thousandth of the effort into my schoolwork, I would have been back in the top classes inside a week.

Of course it would have been easier for everyone if I'd just joined the local swimming club, but I looked more like a piece of driftwood than someone who was capable of surging powerfully through the water. After about a month I abandoned this plan as well. My hair had failed to turn the right golden hue, and I think Dad had started to notice that his chlorine was disappearing.

Despite all that, Leanne Doulton was a turning point in my life. She was the first girl after Helen Edmundson who I was totally in love with and who could elicit from me a reasonably intelligent conversation. Normally I would have found it hard not to vomit from sheer terror. And if it hadn't been for my desire to hurl electrical equipment at her, I would have taken this as a sign of my blossoming maturity.

50

The Write Stuff

I never really got the hang of the seventies. As a child of the sixties, I was rather sad to see my own decade go, coinciding as it did with our leaving England. And I just couldn't take to the seventies at all. In retrospect I'm quite proud of it. "Groovy" was never in my vocabulary. "Flares", "Body-shirt". I didn't say, 'Can I have the new Bay City Rollers album, please?' Didn't get Boz Scaggs, Sherbet (was there ever a lamer group, or a lamer song than *Howzat?*), Peter Frampton and that stupid bagpipe-box thing he had attached to his mouth and guitar. His friends must really pay him out for it now when they drop round for a barbecue. I couldn't take to Dick Emery, Benny Hill, or Paul Hogan—I couldn't find anything funny in women having large breasts. Those supposed disaster movies like *The Towering Inferno*, *Earthquake* (*in Sensurround*, which was such an anticlimax). *The Poseidon Adventure* and all those movies about passenger aircraft running out of fuel, pilots or budget made me cringe.

But the decade is best encapsulated in that song about a prison inmate who writes to his girlfriend and insists that she tie a yellow ribbon around an old oak tree when he gets out. Here we have a guy who's shown no regard for anyone else—he's been away for two years, so, given time off for good behaviour, we're probably talking armed robbery—and yet he feels he can make demands on his long-suffering girlfriend about yellow ribbons, trees and who knows what else. If she had any self-respect, the only thing his girlfriend would be attaching to the tree is a sign in large yellow letters that reads: "STAY ON THE BUS. FORGET ABOUT US. YOU WANKER."

As the seventies came to a close, I wasn't sure whether they were years that had passed me by or I'd passed them by. The whole decade seemed like nothing more than a bridge between my childhood in the sixties and my approaching adulthood in the eighties.

At the end of year 8 I had been relegated from the top stream of students to the middle. I could feel Ray Fearn shaking his head in disapproval wherever he was. Apart from my sketches in Miss Simpson's English class, I had done absolutely no work in my first two years of high school. And if I'd fallen through the educational cracks, I had company. Neil Ollier and Jamie Thorpe had fallen with me. I'd spent two years in the top stream and for some reason I figured that I would now have to spend the next two in the middle. No one had bothered to say that if we got stuck in and did a bit of study, we could move back into the top stream earlier. Neil Ollier had worked it out for himself, though, so when year 10 started he was back up there. Meanwhile Jamie Thorpe and I felt that some of the students we were with still walked with their knuckles dragging along the ground.

I wasn't the class hero, brain, bully, troublemaker, hunk, spunk or chunk. Nor was I the misfit who might turn up with a high-powered rifle and a grievance that went back to kindergarten. I was one of those kids who many people think are there just to make up the numbers—an unpaid extra on the set of everyone else's lives.

If a film had been made about Pendle Hill High School, I would have been buried somewhere in the credits as "Skinny kid with good-looking sister".

So I left. Halfway through year 10 I stood up in the middle of a geography lesson and announced that I'd had enough and was going home. I collected the appropriate form from the office, had my teachers sign it, and walked out of Pendle Hill High and into the future.

As I limped down Binnalong Road for home, I realised that I had totally wasted my four years at high school. I was there to learn and I'd chosen not to. Even though not one single teacher thought to question me about it, the ultimate responsibility rested with me.

I came to the bottom of the hill and stood at the crossroads. As I was waiting for the traffic lights to change, I bent down and felt my knee. It was still swollen and would never regain full mobility. But I still kidded myself that I was destined to be a professional soccer player. The fact that I did eventually manage to achieve this says more about my sheer bloody-mindedness than it does about physiotherapy.

I also thought about my writing, but again came to the conclusion that kids from my background didn't become writers. We might mow their lawns, clean their gutters, fix their cars, but no—we didn't write. I was a working-class boy from Maltby, and we had to know our place.

If writing this book has taught me one thing, however, it is that I became the writer I desperately wanted to be, not despite my background, but because of it.

The lights still hadn't changed. I glanced across at my old junior school, Toongabbie Public. The brick bunker was there at the front gate, despite the fact that school milk had finished long ago. I thought someone should write something about school milk and how awful it was. And someone should write about fascists in beanies, percussion music and how the big kid always got to bang the bass drum while the paste-eater got the cymbals. A poem had to be written, or a sonnet or a play, about Jasmine Robards, Annette Oakley, Indira Narayan, Helen Edmundson and Leanne Doulton, in the "Soft, what light from yonder window breaks?" mould. And what about *Bill and Ben*, Pugsley Porksworth, a visit to the cobbler's, suburban cowboys, or deranged older sisters who decapitate your teddy bear, *and* what about bear-mending wool? What about Maltby, day trips to the seaside with the Loaders, classroom shitters, lollipop men, cocks and cocks-in-waiting, Grandma's bucking bronco teacup, Big Tom's walks, the *Achille Lauro* and grey nurse sharks? Who would commit the Fairy Meadow, the screaming trees, screendoors that went *click-clack*, clotheslines that spun when you turned the handle, Stephen Polecat Flannery, insane roosters, Scottish soldiers and their missing hills, Canberra road trips, the rules for side-garden cricket, red rattlers, and disastrous Easter Hat parades to paper? Someone had to, or they would be lost forever.

I fished in my bag for a pen and a notebook. And when the lights changed, I crossed the road and hobbled home.